EXPLORE WITHIN SELF

FOR MEANING OF LIFE

MANMOHAN CHATURVEDI | PHD

This book is dedicated to my spiritual Guru Shri Vethathiri Maharishi*. The seeds of spirituality sown by His divine self during my formative years have guided me on this journey and by His blessings now I feel ready to share with others the insights gained in this process.

Manmohan Chaturvedi

* Shri Vethathiri Maharishi (1911–2006) was a spiritual leader and founder-trustee of "The World Community Service Centre". Link to his biodata is given below:

https://www.vethathiri.edu.in/pages/vethathiri-maharishi

Contents

Foreword

All of us would like to lead a meaningful life. However, what constitutes a meaningful life is a very amorphous concept. Depending on our stage in life its definition may evolve.

The tribulations of our daily life make us wonder; at some stage, if that is all to life. Constant fear of disease and death compounds our misery and we, having identified with our body and mind, tend to attribute their limitations on us leading to endless confusion.

This book is aimed at providing a primer to the vast field of Spirituality. The author attempts to share his understanding using the Hindu Scriptures as base. The book makes no pretense to be rigorous on the deep Vedantic thoughts and tries to cull out learnings from very basic explanatory texts attributed to Adi Shankaracharya, Patanjali and resource of YouTube videos by eminent spiritual speakers on the topics covered.

I wish great success to this effort at providing easy to use knowledge about our own self and the world around us to the uninitiated in this important aspect of life. This may benefit readers on their Spiritual journey and thus help them find deeper meaning within.

Swami Nikhilananda Saraswati*

Swami Nikhilananda Saraswati, is a Student and a Teacher of Advaita Vedanta. He is a disciple of Swami Chinmayananda Saraswati and Swami Paramananda Bharati. Link to his you tube is given below:

*https://www.youtube.com/channel/ UCE2N0U4JcY9ft2g2cVqqT3g/abou

Preface

For one to be reading this book it is not necessary that one's life lacks meaning. Even if you are on top of life, you may still like to explore the inner side of your personality.

If you, at times, wonder what life really holds for you and are willing to step out of your comfort zone, this book is for you.

We have spent most of our waking hours trying to learn the ropes in the external world. Let us begin our exploration within to find a new meaning of our life.

Our experience of the world during waking hours is based on our five senses and the integrative ability of mind. During sleep, besides deep sleep, the possibility of dream exists, and our mind is the only instrument of this experience as our senses are not functioning during dream experience. During deep sleep devoid of any dreams, the mind is also dormant, and we seem to have no memory of our deep sleep experience on waking up except a feeling that we had a relaxing sleep. Thus, conditioned by the experience of these three states, our association with body and mind is so strong that we perceive them to be our identity. Pain to body and mind is understood as pain to us and all possible efforts are put forth to avoid the source of pain and seek healing. Search for happiness and avoid sorrows is our default mode.

We attempt, through this book, to explore the possibility of going beyond these three known states of experience by our conscious effort. This fourth state is called 'Turiya' a Sanskrit word for numeral four. Our scriptures attach great importance to this experience, and it is known to be experienced by conscious inward travel after shutting down our mental activities and sense perception.

However, success in this process is possible only by regular practice and understanding of the key concepts of our total personality. The payoff is unbelievable; a Self that is intrinsically all knowing, eternal and blissful (Sat, Chid and Anand) is revealed to us and therefore, life assumes a new meaning.

This book is an easy-to-follow guide through the maze of related issues and suggests a prioritized blueprint based on our inherent personality to connect with this aspect of our personality. When we recognize our eternal true nature, all our limitations and insecurities seem to disappear, and Life becomes a continuous celebration.

In this book of fourteen chapters, we devote the first chapter to set the context and subsequent chapters from 2 to 12 are used to familiarize the reader with basic material that may equip him to undertake this inward journey. We use authentic sources to get a nodding acquaintance with the terms of reference and definitions that are crucial for future growth by way of self-study of related scriptures. In chapter 13, we attempt synthesis of the knowledge gained in earlier chapters and in concluding chapter 14 we plan a way forward.

We have shared at the end of book chapter wise links to Online resources, bibliography and three Appendices to provide readers with introductory text on Hindu scriptures combined with 11 main Upanishads, Brahma Sutras and Bhagavad Gita.

The journey is certainly exciting, and we need not be conscious of our lack of time or focus on the initial stages. Once you get a glimpse of what lies within, I can promise you that you will be happy that you began. May God bless you.

Hari Om.

Manmohan Chaturvedi

About The Author

Air Commodore Manmohan Chaturvedi is a retired Indian Air Force Officer. He had interest in Spirituality since college days and was formally initiated in meditation by Shri Vethathiri Maharishi in 1982.

With a purpose to share understanding gathered while reading scriptures and books on philosophy, he is attempting a short book compiled out of posts in his blog 'Search within' with a hope that uninitiated readers may find this basic text useful in their spiritual journey.

Link to the blog 'Search within' is shared below:

https://search-within-self.blogspot.com/2024/06/who-am-i-atma-bodha-knowledge-of-

ONE
SETTING THE CONTEXT

Our experience with this world is full of joys and sorrows. We attempt consciously to avoid sorrows and maximize joys. However, we seem to be helpless in this pursuit. We accept the conditions of life as given and accept, though grudgingly, old age, disease and death. Most of our actions are driven by likes and dislikes. Fear of death is universal in all living beings and we do all that is possible to avoid physical death of our body.

In our childhood and youth, the process of adapting to the world around us and experiencing the thrill of the pleasures that life offers keeps us quite busy. Few instances of personal loss of near and dear ones does bother us but we take them in our stride.

As we approach middle age, our family responsibilities keep us occupied and we try to achieve great success in our career and material wealth creation becomes a cherished goal.

Post retirement most of us wish to enjoy the liberating experience from the work responsibilities and explore those facets of life that we could not because of our work pressures. With age come diseases and disillusionment about the continuance of the happy run of life events. We try to squeeze out worldly pleasures using our aging bodies and join the bandwagon of senior citizens who philosophize that since life is short, we should do everything possible to have our share of happiness. Even the death of our friends and colleagues seems to impel us to feel secretly happy that we have some more time to enjoy this grand event of life.

Very rare persons pause to see the futility of this race for worldly pleasures. With this background of our condition and approach to life, where is the need or time to look for meaning within ?

Most of us when faced with challenges in life approach some form of God for succor. We are generally reconciled to these conditions of life. Very few of us are aware of the existence of this treasure within. Even those who have heard of this treasure and role of it in changing our perspective to life are deterred by the long and arduous path. The maze of issues connected with this discipline and fear of the unknown keeps us on our beaten track.

This book attempts to demystify the wrong notions connected with this inward journey. It also describes the fruits of this journey in terms of our true nature. Effort is made to unbundle various layers of our personality and make it possible to have a glimpse of what we gain by giving up our natural identification with our body and mind. Ability to use body and mind as our tool to experience the hidden facet of our personality that is immortal and all powerful. We have the potential to transform our self-image from the limitations of our body and mind. We would see the world around us through a vision that takes away all our fears. We become God rather than seeking succor from that imaginary entity.

The author has attempted to describe in simple words the world that exists within all of us but very few get a glimpse of it.

TWO
Basic Concepts from Hindu Scriptures

It is important to understand that this inward journey is a leap of faith. Faith denotes our mental state to trust something. In the physical world we use an elevator in a multi-story building, as we have faith about its safe operation. We undertake air travel because of faith in the aviation industry safety norms. Most of our relationships with others are based on faith.

In physical world we are able to evaluate the evidence about the underpinning of our faiths on various things using our senses, mind and intellect. In Spiritual pursuits our senses, mind -intellect system does not seem to help. Our spiritual self is hypothesized to be beyond them and is supposed to be a passive observer of the activities of the physical world including our body-mind complex.

So what is the big deal in connecting with this passive true self? The answer provided by scriptures is that if we change our identification from our body and mind to this spiritual self, many strange things happen. We find that all our sorrows and fears that are rooted in and caused by our body and mind seem to disappear. It is like waking up from a bad dream. The experience is very liberating and persists for all time to come. It is also called Moksha. The reason for our identification with body-mind is ignorance or Avidya, as described in our scriptures. This ignorance can only be removed by knowledge or Jnana.

Thus Jnana (Knowledge)Yoga is the only way through which liberation from ignorance is possible. However, there is a catch; one can practice the Jnana yoga using tool of meditation only if our mind is purified from various past impression that cause continuous turbulence and are roadblocks to our meeting with Spiritual self. So this seems to be a catch 22 situation. How do we get out of it?

In Gita, Krishna provides a blueprint for action. He talks of Karma Yoga at length to Arjun. Some ignorant people mistakenly accuse Him to have put Arjun on the path of War rather than Peace. Arjun wanted to pursue peace at onset of the battle because of his misplaced attachment to relatives in the opposing army.

It is very important to understand nuances of Karma Yoga. Karma Yoga is supposed to act as cleaning agent to our mind and a clean mind is precondition for embarking on Jnana Yoga through meditation practices.

Many approaches for success in Karma Yoga are provided by way of Dos and Don't , in form of Yama and Niyam. Plot is simple. If you want a postgraduate degree you have to start from primary school. If you want to climb a mountain, base camps are a necessary evil. Spirituality does not come easily. We need to have a commitment to our cherished goal and desire to face the challenges in the path.

So this journey needs preparation in terms of understanding background concepts and some behavioral changes to prepare our body and mind. We plan to use the guidance of Indian Vedanta system for this preparation. The Upanishads, the Bhagavad-Gita and the Brahma Sutra constitute the basis of Vedanta. All schools of Vedanta propound their philosophy by interpreting these texts, collectively called the Prasthanatrayi, literally, three sources.

Bhagavad-Gita, which is part of epic Mahabharat is a discourse given by Lord Krishna to Arjun in the battle field and is considered a very renowned source of learning the concepts of Spirituality. Like in battle field of Kurukshetra, in our daily life too we face challenging situations as faced by Arjun. We get confused about our proper reaction to the conflicting stimuli impacting us. In dealing with such dilemma, one is advised to follow one's specified Dharma (Duty). The Bhagavad Gita offers profound insights and guidance on the paths of Karma Yoga (the yoga of action) and Jnana Yoga (the yoga of knowledge).

Some key learnings from the Gita on these two Yogas are given below:

Karma Yoga:

1. Perform actions as a sacred duty without attachment to the fruits of actions (2.47).

2. Work without desire for personal rewards, possessiveness, or egotistical motives (2.49).

3. Equanimity - remain balanced in success and failure, pleasure and pain (2.38).

4. Dedicate all actions to the Divine as an offering without ownership (3.30).

5. Renounce the fruits of actions to attain peace and freedom from bondage (5.12).

6. Work with discipline, without likes and dislikes, for self-purification (18.6).

Jnana Yoga:

1. Discriminate between the temporary material body and the eternal Atman (soul) (2.16).

2. Gain spiritual wisdom by overcoming ignorance and attachments (4.39).

3. Realize the indestructible, immutable, and eternal nature of the Atman (2.20).

4. Understand that the Atman is the true self, distinct from the mind and senses (3.42).

5. Practice meditation, self-study, and contemplation to steady the mind (6.35).

6. Develop equal vision towards all beings, seeing the one Divine in everything (6.29).

7. Conquer the mind and senses through knowledge and detachment (3.43).

8. Attain the supreme knowledge of the imperishable Brahman (the Absolute) (18.50).

Additionally, the Gita emphasizes the harmony of Karma Yoga and Jnana Yoga, where selfless action purifies the mind, leading to spiritual knowledge and eventual liberation. The essence is to act without attachment and perform one's duties with an attitude of offering it to the Divine, while simultaneously cultivating self-knowledge and realizing one's true identity as the eternal Atman.

Meditation

The various approaches to meditation can help us achieve peace of mind and the ability to act with equanimity in the world in the following ways:

1. Concentration/Focused Meditation: This involves techniques like breath awareness, mantra repetition, or gazing at an object. By training the mind to remain focused, we learn to control the wandering tendencies and develop one-pointedness. This helps cultivate mental clarity, stability, and calmness in the face of external circumstances.

2. Mindfulness/Open Monitoring Meditation: Practices like Vipassana or Zen meditation cultivate non-judgmental, present-moment awareness of our thoughts, emotions, and sensations as they arise. This allows us to disengage from ruminative patterns, develop detachment, and respond to situations with more objectivity and equanimity.

3. Loving-Kindness/Compassion Meditation: By cultivating feelings of unconditional love, compassion, and goodwill towards ourselves and others, we overcome negative emotions like anger, hatred, and aversion. This fosters a sense of interconnectedness, empathy, and the ability to act with kindness and equanimity.

4.   **Analytical Meditation**:   Contemplating   profound philosophical teachings or analyzing the nature of the self, impermanence, and interdependence can lead to insights that free us from afflictive mental states and attachments. This wisdom nurtures equanimity and peace.

5. **Devotional Meditation**: By cultivating feelings of love, devotion, and surrender to the Divine/Absolute, we transcend our limited sense of self and develop trust, faith, and inner peace, enabling us to face life's challenges with acceptance and equanimity.

6. **Movement/Embodied Meditation**: Practices like Yoga, Tai Chi, or walking meditation help develop body awareness, grounding, and integration of mind-body. This holistic approach harmonizes our inner state, promoting a sense of centered presence and equanimity.

Across traditions, meditation aims to train the mind, transform our perspective, and help us respond to life's vicissitudes with a balanced, peaceful, and compassionate mindset, ultimately enabling us to act with wisdom and equanimity in the world. However, the above information is of no use to us unless we follow a structured approach to self realization. Panch Kosh Vivek is a technique to be described in chapter 4 that helps us get a perspective.

Patanjali Yoga Sutra provides Ashtanga Yoga (eight limbed Yoga) to help seekers move forward in a systematic manner. We shall describe it too after Panch kosh (Five Layers) Vivek, which attempts to break our personality into five layers to get an idea of our true self.

THREE
CONCEPT OF REBIRTH

Before we can explore concepts of Panch Kosh (Five Sheaths) of our personality, and embark on the journey prescribed by Patanjali in his famous Yoga Sutra, we need to be familiar with the concept of rebirth. Hindu scriptures are very clear about the concept of Moksha which is nothing but cessation of the continuous cycle of rebirth.

Is Moksha really worth pursuing? Many of us are perfectly happy with what life offers; after all it has happy events and sorrows come and go. They may not like the idea of Moksha. It is only those who have developed aversion to the mixed bag that life offers, who are likely to seek Spiritual self. For such seekers, there is assurance that whatever effort is put towards that goal of Moksha does not go waste and the seeker may achieve it over several lifetimes. Every rebirth begins from a higher state and closer to the ultimate goal.

Concept of Rebirth: The philosophy of rebirth or reincarnation (punarjanma) is based on the belief that the soul (atman/jiva) is eternal and undergoes a cycle of birth, death, and rebirth. After death, the subtle body containing the mind, intellect, and impressions (samskaras) carries the cumulative effect of one's karma and becomes the cause for the next incarnation.

The nature and circumstances of the new birth are determined by the cumulative karmas of the previous lives, manifesting as tendencies, abilities, and life situations. Karma is thus the driving force behind the cycle of rebirth (samsara) until one attains moksha (liberation) by exhausting all karmas.

Role of Samskaras: Samskaras refer to the subtle impressions, habitual tendencies, and karmic imprints carried over from previous lives in the form of latent desires and inclinations. These samskaras shape an individual's personality, natural talents, proclivities, and the karmic baggage that determines the nature of rebirth. Samskaras are formed by the countless thoughts, emotions, and actions performed over numerous lifetimes. They act as the subtle driving forces that influence one's behaviors, circumstances, and the path of future incarnations until they are fully resolved or exhausted.

The goal of spiritual practice in Hinduism is to burn or exhaust all accumulated samskaras and karmas through right living, self-discipline, selfless service, and ultimately, the attainment of self-knowledge (atma-jnana) to break free from the cycle of rebirth and attain moksha or liberation. According to Hindu philosophy, our past life samskaras (impressions/tendencies) play a significant role in shaping our current life events and circumstances, while also allowing for the exercise of free will on the spiritual path towards self-realization.

Persistence of Past Life Samskaras: The cumulative impressions and karmic traces (samskaras) from our past lives are carried over into the present birth through the subtle body (linga sharira/ sukshma sharira). These samskaras manifest as innate tendencies, personality traits, inclinations, talents, and even challenges or handicaps we face in this life. They influence our thought patterns, emotional responses, desires, and the karmic situations we encounter, acting as the unseen forces that shape many aspects of our life events. However, samskaras are not viewed as an inescapable destiny, but rather as the starting point or field of play in the present life.

Free Will and Conscious Effort: While past samskaras exert their influence, Hindu scriptures emphasize that human beings possess free will (Sanskrit: purushakara) and the ability to make conscious choices. Through conscious effort, discrimination (viveka), self-discipline (sadacara), and spiritual practice (sadhana), one can gradually overcome negative samskaras and cultivate positive impressions. The practice of karma yoga (selfless action), jnana yoga (path of knowledge), and bhakti yoga (path of devotion) are means to purify the mind and attenuate the hold of past samskaras. Ultimately, it is through the realization of one's true nature as the eternal Self (Atman/Brahman) that one becomes free from the bondage of samskaras altogether.

Shaping Destiny on the Spiritual Path:

On the spiritual path, a sincere seeker is encouraged to exercise free will by making conscious choices that align with dharma (righteous conduct) and lead towards self-realization. Each thought, action, and effort undertaken with awareness and right intention creates new positive samskaras that counteract and gradually erase the negative past impressions.

The guidance of a guru (spiritual teacher) and the study of scriptures help the seeker develop viveka (discriminative wisdom) to navigate the spiritual journey more effectively. Persistent effort, self-effort (purushartha), and the grace of the Divine are considered vital in reshaping one's destiny towards the ultimate goal of moksha (liberation).

Thus, while past life samskaras exert their influence, Hindu thought emphasizes the pivotal role of free will, conscious effort, and spiritual practice in gradually overcoming these karmic impressions and shaping one's destiny towards self-realization and transcendence of all bondage. **Figure 1** attempts to capture this concept. The process is played out iteratively over several life times till one reaches self-realization and subsequent moksha.

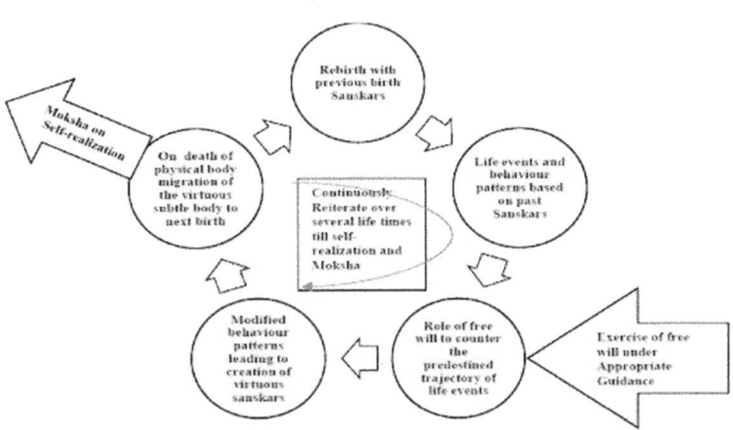

Fig 1: Role of free will to cancel the negative samskaras and Moksha on self-realization

FOUR

WHO AM I REALLY? PANCH KOSHA VIVEK

Hari Om

ब्रह्मविदाप्नोति परम् । तदेषाऽभ्युक्ता । सत्यं ज्ञानमनन्तं ब्रह्म ।

One who knows Brahman, reaches the highest. Satya (reality, truth) is Brahman, Jnana (knowledge) is Brahman, Ananta (infinite) is Brahman. —Taittiriya Upanishad, 2.1.1

In previous chapter 3, we have understood the concept of rebirth and the possibility of escaping this perpetual cycle of birth and death by taking steps under appropriate guidance towards self-realization and eventual Moksha or Nirvana. Now, before we begin this journey towards self-realization, it would be logical to know what our true self is and where to find it. The Taittiriya Upanishad, a revered ancient Hindu scripture, provides us a perspective on our true nature using a process called Panch Kosh (Five Sheath) vivek ; a discrimination method.

The Concept of Ananda: The Taittiriya Upanishad introduces the concept of Ananda, which goes beyond mere happiness or pleasure. It describes Ananda as the inherent bliss that permeates all existence, beyond the realm of fleeting emotions. The Upanishad encourages us to seek this eternal bliss by realizing our true nature, transcending the limitations of the material world.

The Five Sheaths (Pancha Koshas): The Taittiriya Upanishad presents the idea of Pancha Koshas, the five sheaths that envelop the true self. These sheaths include the physical body, vital energy, the mind, intellect, and the blissful core of being. By understanding and transcending these layers, one can delve deeper into their true essence and establish a profound connection with the divine. The true self is beyond all the five sheaths including Anandmaya kosha or blissful core.

Anandmaya kosha is our staging stage for self realization of true self. One does not stay at this blissful core and by developing detachment to this blissful layer too, we transcend to the ultimate goal of self realization. This process is akin to peeling layers of an onion. So what do we find at the core of the onion? Really nothing that we can see. Similarly when we start peeling these layers of our personality using the Panch Kosh vivek process, we don't find any object as our true self. So is the search futile ? Not really. Our true self is the one who is actually doing the peeling. It is aware of all the five layers. It is the observer of these five layers. It is the consciousness itself.

All the five layers are manifestations of that true self and function only because of the core of consciousness within. All layers of the onion are a manifestation of onion only. Similarly, all aspects (sheaths) of our personality are manifestations of the spiritual self. The waves of the ocean are the ocean itself; all are full of water. All ornaments are nothing but gold.

Figure 1 attempts to describe our journey from body consciousness to realization of our true nature (Atma) by transcending the five koshas or layers of body-mind apparatus.

Figure 2 is attempting to show pictorially the inter-relationship of five sheaths; with gross level Annamaya Kosha (our physical body) being the outermost ring and subtler constituents are reached as we move inward. The true self (Atman) is at the very core.

Fig 1: Process of Panch Kosha Vivek to realization of Self

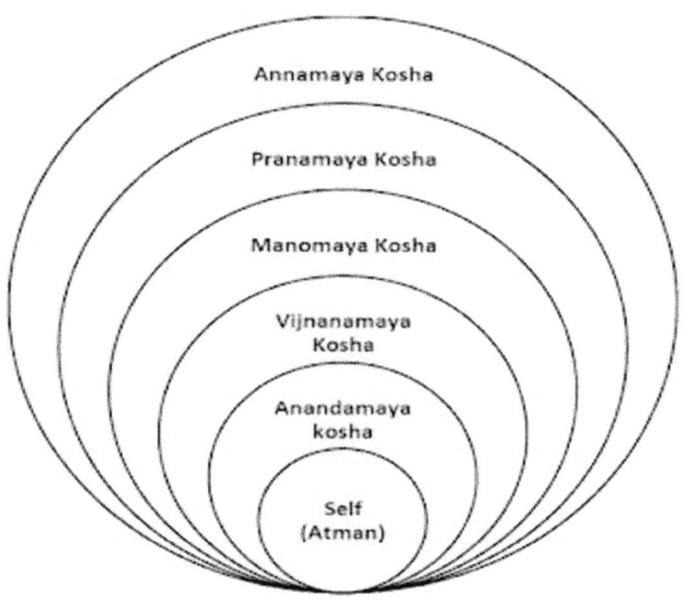

Fig 2: The pictorial view of five Sheaths that constitute our personality

The teaching of Pancha Kosha Viveka states that the true Self (Atman) is distinct from these five sheaths or coverings. These sheaths veil or obscure the realization of the Atman. The goal of self-realization is to transcend each of these sheaths or layers of existence, and ultimately realize one's true identity through the blissful Anandamaya Kosha - the Atman, which is one with Brahman (the Absolute Reality).

The process of PanchKosh Vivek involves:

(a) Recognizing each sheath for what it is through discrimination (viveka). We need to read scriptures, listen to people who have the ability to guide us and introspect in silence. The process is slow and tedious but certainly worth the effort.

(b) Withdrawing identification from each outer sheath as "not the Self." One key attribute of our True Self is that it is changeless. All sheaths that are manifested out of it are changing with time. Our body ages, our mind changes at a pace that is phenomenal, our intellect too changes. A Goldsmith during evaluation of gold ornaments' value is looking at the gold substrate only; he can create different designs of ornaments but gold is changeless. The value is of Gold. Likewise, value is of changeless Self.

(c) Steadily moving inward until one realizes the bliss sheath of pure consciousness as one's true nature. As we move forward, we experience subtler aspects of our personality. The happiness that we experience in our day to day existence ; be it from a good meal or other body pleasures, all are nothing but trickles from this bliss sheath. If we can remain in bliss sheath continuously, we go through life in a state of flow. By peeling off these sheaths, one moves from ignorance (avidya) to Self-knowledge (Atma Jnana). The source of our ignorance is to seek permanence in a changing world. The difference between unchanging (Sat) and changing (Asat) has to be understood by deep contemplation. Journey of Self realization is to develop ability to discriminate 'Sat' from 'Asat'. The Upanishads guide the seeker to look within and directly experience in the Anandamaya Kosha - the blissful Self that is eternal, changeless, and one with the ultimate Brahman. It is to be clearly understood that Anandmaya kosha is only a staging ground for self realization and one has to go beyond it to reach ultimate goal of liberation.

This knowledge is helpful for a seeker as it puts the things in perspective. However, one has to follow a structured approach to achieve this goal of blissful experience. Rishi Patanjalli through his famous Yoga Sutra has provided the steps necessary towards self realization using Ashtanga Yoga (Eight Limbed Yoga). We shall try to understand the key facets of this Yoga Sutra over next few chapters.

In The Journal of Transpersonal Psychology, 2016, Vol. 48, No. 2, Maharaj K. Raina in his article "THE LEVELS OF HUMAN CONSCIOUSNESS AND CREATIVE FUNCTIONING: INSIGHTS FROM THE THEORY OF PANCHA KOSHA (FIVE SHEATHS OF CONSCIOUSNESS)", describes these sheaths very elaborately and the following text is an adaption from this article.

Annamaya kosha The outermost layer, the Annamaya kosha, the food sheath or 'food body,' is a representation of the gross physical body, considered as primitive and the least powerful part of the persona. This sheath is regarded as the medium of enjoyment for gross objects through the physical senses. All living beings in this world are born from food and remain alive by the consumption of food. It is the external body, made of matter, like other objects seen outside by our gross senses. Here, matter is called 'food', thus conceiving it organically. This sheath is concerned with our physical existence: birth, growth, change, death and decay are its qualities.

Pranamaya Kosha The second covering of the Self is the pranamaya kosha or vital sheath consisting of the five pranas or vital energies and the five karma indriyas or organs of action. This level of being is associated with the breath, the prana, and the fundamental lifeforce. It is also associated with feelings, the emotions. This is a template of concentrated life force (prana). Prana, in its universal aspect, underlies all physical and mental processes. It stands specifically for the field of energy that penetrates and surrounds the physical body and has variously been styled 'astral body,' 'etheric double,' and 'plasma body.' It is the medium of exchange in the whole psychophysiological system. Prana is the life force of the persona responsible for the various physiological functions within the body, and it plays a critical role as the mediating link between body and mind. In the conscious state one experiences prana, when it is manifested in the form of the breath . Here, energy is also described as prana, which means 'living breath.' The Upanishads prescribe various meditations on prana to raise consciousness from the body to a higher level of the life force. Those who can identify with this powerhouse of energy attain great control over the body; they spontaneously experience a new feeling of freedom, strength, and joy. Consciousness on the level of the Pranamaya kosha is more subtle and powerful than that of the first covering, the Annamaya kosha.

Manomaya Kosha Next is the level of living energy, the mental sheath, the Manomaya kosha or the 'covering of mind', the emotional body or what Vedanta calls the mind. This level of mental activity is commonly captured in the Sanskrit term manas (from the verbal root man, meaning "to think"). The manas is the sensory-motor mind, which thrives on the material gathered from the senses of hearing, touch, sight, taste, and smell. This sheath deals with the emotional, mental or perceptual part of the body, which comprises not just the mind, but also the organs within the body. Its functions relate to perceptual organization. It is the level that receives impulses from the external world through the senses, organizes the sensory data, processes thoughts, emotions, and meaningful patterns, influences the Prana kosha, and channels the ways one thinks. The Manomaya kosha is where thinking and doubting occurs. This is the conceiving intellect, made up of thoughts that interpret the patterns of activity that the senses perceive. Thus interpreted, these patterns are conceived as meaningful information, about an intelligible world. This kosha is where all thoughts originate: the doubts, the anger, the lust, the exhilaration, the depression and the delusion. This kosha represents inventive, critical thought: the making of novel connections, the combination of ideas.

Vijnanamaya Kosha Identified with "higher" mental functions, often expressed in the term buddhi that consists of the intellect (thoughts), the ego (sense of individuality), and the chitta (informational memory), Vijnanamaya kosha, represents not only 'cognition' but also 'intellect' and 'wisdom.' Vijnana means "certain knowledge"; it includes the three mental activities of feeling, willing, and knowing. It also represents the mind, skill and all the intelligence behind human work. This sheath represents the intelligence or the consciousness that is the discriminative part of the mind underneath the processing, thinking aspect of mind. It knows, decides, judges, and discriminates. This is the organ of philosophical thought and metaphysical intuition. It is also the seat of the human will, by which one orients life toward either unreflective bodily experience or enhanced awareness and spiritual realization. The Manomaya and Vijnanamaya sheaths together constitute what is called the mind. First there is Manomaya thought, which is on a level above mere physical or emotional reaction, but is still based on complex manipulations of ideas derived from the physical world. Manomaya kosha is the gross level of mind comprising emotions, thoughts, and different types of feelings and has no capacity to discriminate between right and wrong deeds according to situations. The Vijnanamaya kosha governs the gross mind to take appropriate decisions with knowledge that has been accrued through various means. It is based on taking intuitions from the upper realms and using them to guide one's feelings and actions. In the first, the reflexes are in control; in the second, one's higher intuitions are in control.

Anandamaya Kosha Bliss is not a static feeling but rather dynamic and unlimited, flowing uninterruptedly out of Consciousness. Anandamaya kosha, the blissful sheath, is the most interior of the kosha, the first of the koshas surrounding the Atman, the eternal center of consciousness. When one transcends all the previous layers, one is in bliss with life. Bliss is the highest dimension of our existence. It is a state of being in which one can detach oneself from the emotions and live in perfect health of body and mind. This is the most harmonious state of mind possible, associated with states of ecstasy and rapture. Many Yoga devotees, many Yoga masters and the Buddha and other spiritual masters lived this existence in a state of bliss and acquired much knowledge through the power of meditation and dis-identification with the external self. This is a state characterized by positive feeling, which is not dependent on any object or events of external reality. Thus, the "experience of ananda, bliss, is a qualitatively different sense of positive state and well being from that is associated with other sheaths, koshas. Also called the Causal layer and considered as the deepest and most subtle in human personality, this layer forms the subtlest of sheaths . It is the co-coordinating layer of personality, with the word ananda or 'happiness' being used in the sense of 'harmony', 'integration', and complete satisfaction or fulfillment, the experience one has when completely free from any kind of stress or disharmony, conflicts or compulsions, needs, drives, or anxieties. This kosha is not bound by either time or space. This is the body one enters whenever a desire is fulfilled and also in the thought-free state characteristic of nirvikalpa samadhi and, more familiarly, deep sleep. When used by Buddhists and the Vedic sages who preceded them, bliss (Ananda) is the vibrancy of creation, the underlying dynamism that enters the world as vitality, desire, ecstasy, and joy. Anandamaya kosha can be described as the transcendental body, and the experience of this state is sometimes taken as the highest ascent of mystical experience, an experience of total transcendence or the blissful body. Ananda is the natural innate state of the conscious being and can remain elusive unless one follows righteous actions with the right attitudes as dictated by conscience and discriminative faculty. It is Anandamaya kosha that dissolves the veil of the mind leading to ecstasy, bliss and what Maslow calls "integrated creativity" from which "comes the great work of art, or philosophy or science" (Maslow, 1968, p. 142). These qualities correspond to the higher ranks in Maslow's hierarchy of needs, low levels of narcissism, and a high degree of personal integration. It is when in Anandamaya state that one connects to consciousness resulting in transcendental awareness, transcending the ordinary limits of the physical world and experiencing spiritual states of consciousness.

Conclusion: So by practicing Panch Kosh vivek, we can get an overall view of our true self. Our body identification gives way to identification of our whole self and not parts thereof. We rightly say that body , mind and intellect are only my parts and function because of me. Death of the body is not my death. Any damage to my ornaments is not damage to the substrate of gold. A new ornament would manifest out of the core gold.

FIVE

JOURNEY TOWARDS OUR TRUE SELF -THE PATANJALI YOGA SUTRA

Hari Om

असतो मा साद गमय, तमसो मा ज्योतिर् गमय, मृत्योर मा अमृतम् गमय

(Asato Ma Sad Gamaya, Tamaso Ma Jyotir Gamaya, Mrityor Ma Amritam Gamaya)

Lead us from ignorance to truth, Lead us from darkness to light, Lead us from death to deathlessness.

- Brihadaranyaka Upanishad

In previous chapter, using Panch Kosh vivek method, an attempt was made to unbundle our personality; starting from physical body as we move inward our ultimate goal is to get a glimpse of true spiritual self.

What is the motivation for undertaking this journey?

Those of us interested to rise above pains and sorrow by acquiring a detached perspective towards life events could be the possible candidates.

There are alternatives to this journey. We may seek support of a personal God to help us tide over difficult patches by sincere devotion and accept whatever we face in life as His will. This would constitute Bhakti yoga approach. All major religions of the world ; be it Christianity, Islam or Hindu, seem to have a construct about all powerful God with various attributes that are super human and provide the devotee a sense of security as one goes through life. For life after death also many concepts like Paradise, Jannat and Swarg exist that tend to modulate our behavior while alive.

However, Vedic approach to the mystery of life has slightly different approach. It propounds that the ultimate cause of this universe is an impersonal, Conscious being called Brahman. It goes on to suggest that the individual being (Jiva) at one's core is either a small part or whole of Brahman. However, because of ignorance (Avidya), Jiva is unable to relate with this Brahman. This individual being (Jiva) faces happiness and sorrows in present life based on the past life samskaras.

The above concepts of rebirth and theory of Karma is based on the four Vedas, a body of knowledge believed to be manifested by the Creator of this world to ancient Rishis (seekers of knowledge) during their spiritual quest.

Knowledge portions (Jnana Kand) of the four Vedas also called Upanishads, have deep insights about the nature of this world and its Creator.

Brahma Sutras, attributed to Sage Ved Vyas, is an attempt to cull out this sacred wisdom. The Brahma Sutras later became basis for very structured commentaries by other Rishis and gave birth to Samkhya philosophy that started with a concept of duality i.e. Brahman and Jiva being independent entities. Rishi Kapila, its proponent, stipulates eternal existence of sentient Soul (Brahman, or Purusha) and insentient Nature (Prakriti or Maya). All worldly creations are the result of a relationship established between these two.

While various offshoots of Brahma Sutras like Samkhya, Advaita or Vishisht Advaita are philosophical constructs that differ from each other in certain nuances, they continue to coexist with healthy debate to know the ultimate reality. These are open systems and unlike various religions including Hindu Sanatan Dharma, do not consider personal God as the center feature. While religions are useful in managing societies and impose some discipline in the behavior of masses, at times, religions and cults emanating from them are known to be the cause of conflict.

Faith is the central theme of religions and cults. It tends to bring conformist tendencies in the practitioner and may not appeal to rationality of many, particularly with the spread of scientific temper in current world societies. The vedantic systems being open ended and suggesting an impersonal Creator of this world may be more to the liking of scientific temper. Uptake of spirituality in modern time is an indication of its growing popularity.

While describing the concept of rebirth as per Hindu scriptures, we had indicated the possibility of one realizing one's true self by following a structured path under guidance of a suitable person who has already undertaken this journey of Self realization and is available in physical form as his destined karmas (Prarabdha Karma) are still not exhausted so he cannot drop his gross physical body.

In Hindu thoughts, Patanjali yoga sutra is considered to be one structured approach towards realization of our true self. As a departure from the philosophical theories, it attempts to provide us a stage by stage blueprint for action.

No affiliation with any religion is necessary. Any person interested in this self-discovery journey can get on board. However, there are essential steps that need to be taken. These are universal in nature and there cannot be any short cut.

According to Patanjalli, the key goal of the journey is to still (calm down) our mental tendencies (Chitta Vrati). When our highest mind layer called 'Chitta' is perfectly still with no tendencies perturbing it, one gets a realization of one's true self.

It is akin to viewing the image of a full moon in the calm water of a lake. The lake is like our Chitta and viewing the moon is the process of self-realization.

This process of stilling or calming the Chitta and viewing our true self can only be understood by undertaking the journey.

As our mental faculties are already dropped on the way towards the final goal of self-realization (Samadhi), it is impossible to describe it by a realized seeker. Words fail him; so to say. It can only be alluded to and hence guidance by a suitable teacher is recommended.

However, it is a very personal, life changing experience that alters our self-image permanently and one goes through life after this self-realization, with equanimity under pleasure and pain.

The Yoga Sutras of Patanjali provide a comprehensive blueprint for self-realization and spiritual enlightenment. The main purpose of yoga is to learn to control our mind and not be controlled by our thoughts. Through yoga we learn to dissociate from our thoughts.

The teachings and practices of the Yoga Sutras are based on three principles:

1) Suffering is not caused by forces outside of us but by our faulty and limited perception of life and of who we are. Suffering is not caused by the situation, but by our thoughts about the situation.

2) The unwavering peace we seek is realized by experiencing the unlimited and eternal peace that is our true identity. Though hidden by our ignorance, it exists within us, waiting to be revealed. Peace exists within us.

3) Peace and self-realization is attained by mastering the mind. Only a single-pointed, calm mind can reveal the true self.

There are 196 sutras (aphorisms) presented in four chapters (or padas). Each pada emphasizes a different aspect of the science of yoga.

Patanjali divided his Yoga Sutras into 4 chapters or books (Sanskrit pada), containing in all 196 aphorisms (Sutras), divided as follows:

Pada 1: Concentration (Samadhi Pada)

Pada 2: Practice (Sadhana Pada)

Pada 3: Experiences (Vibhuti Pada)

Pada 4: Absolute Freedom (Kaivalya Pada)
The Eight Limbs of Yoga (Ashtanga Yoga):

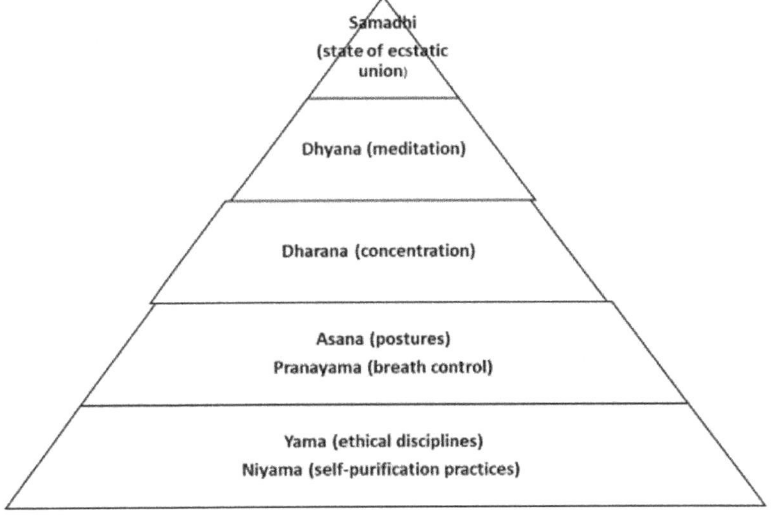

Figure 1: Hierarchy of Eight Limbs of Yoga

The Yoga Sutras outline an eight-fold path known as Ashtanga Yoga, which serves as a systematic approach to self-realization. **Figure 1** describes the hierarchy of these limbs. The end objective of Samadhi or Self Realization is achieved only after the remaining seven underlying stages are firmly established. Yama and Niyam are the foundational attributes and are at the same level. Similarly, Asan and Pranayama are shown at the same level as they relate to our body.

These eight limbs are as given below:

Yama (ethical disciplines)

1. Ahimsa (non-violence)
2. Satya (truthfulness)
3. Asteya (non-stealing)
4. Brahmacharya (moderation of the senses/right use of energy)

5. Aparigraha (non-greed)

Niyama (self-purification practices)

1. Saucha (cleanliness) Saucha can be translated as 'cleanliness', but it doesn't just mean physical cleanliness
2. Santosha (contentment)
3. Tapas (discipline)
4. Svadhyaya (self study)
5. Isvara Pranidhana (surrendering to a higher power)
6. Asana (postures)

Pranayama (breath control)
Pratyahara (sense withdrawal)
Dharana (concentration)
Dhyana (meditation)
Samadhi (state of ecstatic union)

Stilling the Modifications of the Mind:
A central tenet of the Yoga Sutras is that the goal is to calm the fluctuations of the mind (chitta vritti nirodhah). By quieting the constant chatter and distractions of the mind, one can experience the true nature of the Self or Purusha.

The Practice of Kriya Yoga:
Patanjali outlines a three-part process called Kriya Yoga, which consists of tapas (austerity/discipline), svadhyaya (self-study), and Ishvara pranidhana (surrender to the Divine). This practice purifies the body, mind, and spirit, preparing the individual for self-realization.

The Contemplation of Ishvara (The Lord):
The Yoga Sutras recommend the contemplation of Ishvara, or the Lord, as a means to attain the highest form of Samadhi (union). This can be achieved through devotion, repetition of sacred words (mantras), or contemplation on the qualities of the Divine.

The Removal of Afflictions (Kleshas):

Patanjali identifies five afflictions (kleshas) that hinder self-realization: ignorance (avidya), egoism (asmita), attachment (raga), aversion (dvesha), and clinging to life (abhinivesha). The Yoga Sutras provide methods to overcome these obstacles.

The Development of Discriminative Discernment (Viveka Khyati):

Viveka Khyati, or discriminative discernment, is the ability to distinguish between the eternal Purusha (Self) and the temporary Prakriti (material world). This insight is essential for self-realization.

By systematically following the eight limbs, practicing Kriya Yoga, contemplating the Divine, removing afflictions, and developing discriminative discernment, the Yoga Sutras of Patanjali provide a comprehensive framework for attaining the ultimate goal of self-realization and union with the Divine.

The video links given as resources give background information about Patanjalli Rishi and basic outline of the Yoga Sutra.

We shall attempt to provide more insights about the eight limbs of this Yoga Sutra in succeeding chapters.

SIX

HOW TO BEGIN THE INWARD JOURNEY? SADHNA ESSENTIALS

Hari Om Tat Sat

(The manifest reality, this world, is represented by the mantra 'Hari'. 'Om' is the unmanifest reality, the unseen, invisible, uncreated aspect of the absolute. So, 'Hari Om Tat Sat' means 'That is Truth'. That which I see with my eyes and that which is beyond my eyes are both the same, not different.)

Having decided to undertake an inward journey with potential benefit of realizing our true self, we look at Patanjali's Yoga sutras.We had acquired an overview of Patanjali Yoga Sutras in previous chapter 5. The four chapters or padas of these Sutras have different focuses.

For a beginner, practice of Sadhna pada is considered essential. It prepares our body and mind to undertake the final three stages viz. Dharna, Dhyan and Samadhi of the eight limbs of Ashtanga yoga.

These final stages require our body and mind to be purified by going through Kriya yoga. This Kriya yoga essentially covers the first five steps of the eight limbs of yoga sutra.

The practice of Yama (ethical disciplines) and Niyama (self-purification practices) are akin to Ten Commandments of Christianity.

The 5 components each of Yama and Niyama support a three-part process called Kriya Yoga, which consists of tapas (austerity/discipline), svadhyaya (self-study), and Ishvara pranidhana (surrender to the Divine). This practice purifies the body and mind preparing the individual for self realization.

For ease of recall these eight limbs are as given below:

Yama (ethical disciplines)

1. Ahimsa (non-violence)
2. Satya (truthfulness)
3. Asteya (non-stealing)
4. Brahmacharya (moderation of the senses/right use of energy)
5. Aparigraha (non-greed)

Niyama (self-purification practices)

1. Saucha (cleanliness) Saucha can be translated as 'cleanliness', but it doesn't just mean physical cleanliness
2. Santosha (contentment)
3. Tapas (discipline)
4. Svadhyaya (self study)
5. Isvara Pranidhana (surrendering to a higher power)
6. Asana (postures)

    Pranayama (breath control)
    Pratyahara (sense withdrawal)
    Dharana (concentration)
    Dhyana (meditation)
    Samadhi (state of ecstatic union)

The Practice of Kriya Yoga:

Patanjali outlines a three-part process called Kriya Yoga, which consists of tapas (austerity/discipline), svadhyaya (self-study), and

Ishvara pranidhana (surrender to the Divine). This practice purifies the body, mind, and spirit, preparing the individual for self realization.

The Contemplation of Ishvara (The Lord):

The Yoga Sutras recommend the contemplation of Ishvara, or the Lord, as a means to attain the highest form of Samadhi (union). This can be achieved through devotion, repetition of sacred words (mantras), or contemplation on the qualities of the Divine.

The Removal of Afflictions (Kleshas):

Patanjali identifies five afflictions (kleshas) that hinder self realization: ignorance (avidya), egoism (asmita), attachment (raga), aversion (dvesha), and clinging to life (abhinivesha). The Yoga Sutras provide methods to overcome these obstacles.

The Development of Discriminative Discernment (Viveka Khyati):

Viveka Khyati, or discriminative discernment, is the ability to distinguish between the eternal Purusha (Self) and the temporary Prakriti (material world). This insight is essential for self realization.

By systematically following the eight limbs, practicing Kriya Yoga, contemplating the Divine, removing afflictions, and developing discriminative discernment, the Yoga Sutras of Patanjali provide a comprehensive framework for attaining the ultimate goal of self realisation and union with the Divine.

There are a total of 55 Sutras in Sadhna Pada. These Sutras essentially attempt to act as a guide to the seeker on this inward journey by describing various roadblocks and practical ways to overcome them. End result of continuous and dedicated practice is purification of body and mind, resulting in the ability to practice Concentration and Meditation effectively. The key attributes of this ability are detachment from worldly pleasures and consistent practice. Constant and long duration practice of these two techniques may lead the seeker to self realization.

It may be observed that the first five limbs starting from Yama/Niyamas up to Pratyahara (sense withdrawal)or the Kriya yoga are focussing on external part of the seeker's personality.However, without this tuning of external dimension of our personality the final two stages leading to Samadhi (Self Realization) are impossible.

Thus a holistic approach is necessary.By following the eight limbs of yoga, individuals synchronize their mind, body, and soul. Each limb builds upon the others, creating a holistic approach to self-realization and inner harmony. Through ethical conduct, physical postures, breath control, and meditation, practitioners can deepen their spiritual connection, quiet the mind, and experience profound states of awareness and bliss.

Certain practical suggestions for practicing Yamas and Niyamas in our daily life are given below.

1. Yamas (Ethical Guidelines):

- Non-Violence (Ahimsa):

- In daily life, a seeker can practice ahimsa by avoiding harm to others physically, emotionally, or verbally.

- Real-world example: Choosing not to engage in gossip or spreading rumours about someone.

- Truthfulness (Satya):

- Seekers can practice satya by being honest and transparent.

- Real-world example: When asked about their opinion, a seeker refrains from exaggerating or distorting the truth.

- Non-Stealing (Asteya):

- Asteya involves not taking what doesn't belong to us.

- Real-world example: A seeker respects intellectual property rights and avoids piracy or plagiarism.

- Continence (Brahmacharya):

- Brahmacharya is about moderation and channeling energy appropriately.

- Real-world example: A seeker practices moderation in food, entertainment, and relationships.

- Non-Greed (Aparigraha):

- Aparigraha encourages detachment from material possessions.

- Real-world example: A seeker donates unused items to charity rather than hoarding them.

2. Niyamas(Personal Observances):

- Cleanliness (Saucha):
- Saucha involves physical and mental purity.
- Real-world example: A seeker maintains a clean-living space and practices hygiene.
- Contentment (Santosha):
- Santosha is about finding contentment regardless of external circumstances.
- Real-world example: A seeker appreciates what they have instead of constantly desiring more.
- Self-Discipline (Tapas):
- Tapas refers to inner strength and willpower.
- Real-world example: A seeker wakes up early for meditation even when tempted to sleep in.
- Self-Study (Svadhyaya):
- Svadhyaya involves introspection and self-reflection.
- Real-world example: A seeker regularly journals their thoughts and emotions.
- Devotion to a Higher Power (Ishvara Pranidhana):
- Ishvara pranidhana is surrendering to a divine force.
- Real-world example: A seeker practices gratitude and acknowledges a higher purpose in life.

3. Integration into Daily Life:

- Seekers can integrate these principles into their routines:
- Morning Practice: Begin the day with meditation, expressing gratitude, and setting intentions.
- Mindful Actions: Throughout the day, practice mindfulness in interactions, speech, and actions.
- Evening Reflection: Reflect on how well you embodied the yamas and niyamas during the day.

Remember that these ethical guidelines and personal observances are not rigid rules but flexible principles. Seekers adapt them to their unique circumstances, always striving for self-improvement and inner growth.

SEVEN

SAMADHI PROCESS - HOW THE TRUE SELF IS REACHED?

Hari Om Tat Sat

अहं ब्रह्मास्मि

(I am the Absolute)

In our search for our true identity we have taken help from Patanjali yoga Sutras. After having an overview of these sutras in Chapter 5 and looking at the preparations needed on this path in Chapter 6, we are attempting to get familiar with the actual process that may lead to union with our divine nature , formally called Samadhi.

The other two chapters (Padas) i.e. Vibhuti Pada and Kaivalya Pada are focusing on the description of the super natural powers and state of liberation that a realized seeker experiences. These two padas are planned to be covered later and they, unlike Sadhana pada, do not directly contribute to the goal of self-realization but are a consequence of self-realization.

It may be surprising to many of us but we all have been experiencing a state of Samadhi on a daily basis during dreamless deep sleep.

Our mind and senses are suspended in deep sleep and the only observer of that state is our true self. However, the absence of mind during this process inhibits us from recalling details of that state.

We have a vague feeling of having enjoyed that state after we wake up and as we all know, sleep is essential for our continued wellbeing.

So, we connect with our true self on a regular basis. The fact of the matter is that our true conscious self is the ONLY observer of all our worldly experiences.

Our mind, senses and body are just plain inert matter being made to appear live by the power of the conscious self.

During Samadhi we attempt a voluntary reunion with this true self by process of meditation. Thus, meditation is essential for realizing our true self.

Even in Bhakti (Devotion) yoga the ultimate union with Divine is considered to be meditative surrender of our limited self to the Divine within.

Samadhi is actually a fourth state also called Turiya (numeral 4 in Sanskrit) in which we enter while fully awake by a process of stilling the perturbations in our mind. The other three are our waking, dream and deep sleep states.

Samadhi is deemed to have taken place when our mind is completely still, much like the placid water of a clean lake, reflecting the Moon from the night sky. The Moon is our true self.

There is no hard boundary separating the two phases viz. Sadhna and Samadhi. The eight limbs of Ashtanga Yoga consists of the first preparatory steps connected with our self and the environment we live in.

They are preparations to ensure that we progress smoothly through Dharna (Concentration) and Dhyan (Meditation). Effective meditation increases our possibility to get a glimpse of divinity within. **Figure 1** attempts to capture this process towards self-realization.

This process entails a very high proportion of actual practice. Like Cycling, Swimming or Dancing can not be learnt by watching

YouTube videos alone and actual practice is necessary, same is the case with Yoga.

This spiritual journey of a seeker can be understood by a metaphor of an Aircraft getting airborne.

Preparatory Sadhna is akin to the ground crew working on it to ensure it's airworthiness. The process of taxiing to the runway takeoff point is like Dharna.

The takeoff run with full throttle is equivalent to Dhyan. Only when an aircraft reaches a critical speed can it get unstuck from the runway and get airborne. Similarly, the Dhyan has to be firm to reach the Samadhi stage.

Once airborne aircraft gets over its earlier limitations of not being able to travel across unpaved lands, rivers or mountains. Similarly, a seeker in Samadhi stage transcends the earlier limitation of his mind and experiences a new found freedom or liberation.

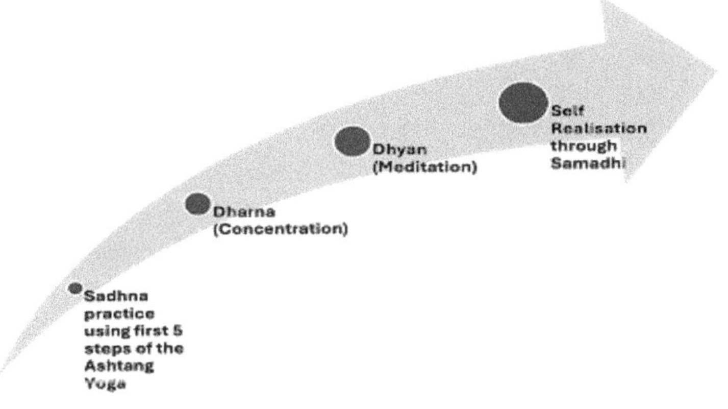

Figure 1: Process towards Self-Realization

It is observed that a seeker may have apprehension in following the preparatory phase of observance of five Yamas, five Niyamas, stabilizing of Asan (Physical Exercises to strengthen the body), Pranayama (Breathing Exercises) and Pratyahara (Withdrawal of senses from world objects).

It is recommended that a seeker may motivate oneself to take the initial baby steps on this path, by appreciation of the immense value that the glimpse of the divine within provides them at the end of the long tunnel of spiritual Sadhna.

Another factor that inhibits us on this path is the fear of the unknown. The very idea of losing our existing concept of self to a very nebulous construct of divine self and consequences of this transformation on our 'business as usual' life, acts as a damper.

However, this fear is totally unfounded. A realized person is able to lead life with much better control on their interactions with the world around them. Many insecurities and dissipation of our energies in useless pursuits give way to a more holistic approach to life and our relations with others including our immediate family and friends become better.

Having allayed these fears of the seeker, we may take a brief look at the actual process. Though this journey is a personal quest, the need of a teacher/guide (Guru) to guide is emphasized. Even for the Sadhna phase, the role of a suitable guide or a course of instruction is highly recommended.

Like in any discipline, the need to have our concepts clarified through self-study (Svadhyaya) and reflection (Manan) is essential to get the critical mass of detachment (Vairagya) from worldly indulgences. Future posts would attempt to provide relevant information as considered necessary for a seeker.

Yoga Sutra, is one of the most detailed maps of higher consciousness; it deals primarily with the nature of mind, and with how mind is transformed through different stages of samadhi (higher consciousness) until the liberated state, or kaivalya, finally appears.

Samadhi Pada is the opening chapter of Patanjali's Yog-Darshan or Yoga Sutras. It consists of 51 sutras that delve into the concept of enlightenment and the path to self-realization.

The term "samadhi" refers to a state of deep concentration, meditation, and absorption where the individual's consciousness merges with the object of focus. In this state, the sense of separation between the observer and the observed dissolves, leading to profound inner realization.

Purpose of Yoga According to Samadhi Pada:

Patanjali explains that the purpose of yoga is to quiet the fluctuations of the mind, known as "vrittis."

These mental fluctuations are the source of restlessness, distractions, and suffering.

By practicing yoga, one aims to still these mental fluctuations and experience the true nature of the self beyond the conditioned mind.

Chitta-Vritti-Nirodha: Stilling the Mind:

• A central concept in Samadhi Pada is "chitta-vritti-nirodha," which refers to the stilling or calming of the mind-stuff (chitta).

• Through various yogic practices, the seeker learns to quiet the mind, allowing it to settle into a state of stillness and clarity.

Overcoming Obstacles:

• The chapter discusses obstacles and distractions that hinder the attainment of samadhi. These include desires, attachments, aversions, and other mental disturbances.

• Patanjali presents a path for overcoming these obstacles through the practice of "abstinences" (yamas) and "observances" (niyamas).

Types of Samadhi:

1. Savikalpa Samadhi:

o In this state, the mind is concentrated and still, but the merger with the object of focus is not yet complete.

o The practitioner experiences a deep meditative absorption, but there is still a subtle sense of duality.

2. Nirvikalpa Samadhi:

o This is the highest state of samadhi.

o The mind is fully absorbed and merged with the object of focus, leading to a complete dissolution of the sense of self.

o In Nirvikalpa Samadhi, the seeker experiences oneness and unity with the divine or the true self.

Importance of Samadhi:

• Samadhi is considered the crowning achievement of yogic practice. It represents the apex of the yogic journey, where the seeker transcends ordinary consciousness and enters a state of profound realization.

• Attaining samadhi is crucial for achieving liberation (moksha) and self-realization.

In summary, Samadhi Pada establishes the fundamental principles of yoga, emphasizing the quieting of the mind and the practice of samadhi as a means to realize the true self. It invites seekers to explore the depths of their consciousness and experience the ultimate union with existence.

A practical guide to this important topic of Samadhi as a resource, a link to YouTube videos play list of 11 videos by Swami Nikhilananda Saraswati is included in the online resource section.

These videos are a very authentic source of relevant information with examples from everyday life. Day 8 session has audio loss after about 20 minutes and viewers may switch to day 9 session without any noticeable discontinuity as in each session a recap of previous session is provided.

It is highly recommended that seekers may patiently listen to this set of 11 videos as convenient to get a grasp of this abstract topic. Practical experience of meditation would reinforce the key concepts brought out by a very accomplished speaker and immensely help the seeker in his journey.

EIGHT

SPIRITUAL POWERS OF A YOGI - VIBHUTI PADA

Hari Om Tat Sat

Previous two Chapters 6 and 7 have attempted to get a familiarity on the Sadhna and Samadhi aspects of Yoga practice.

The Vibhuti Pada, also known as the "Portion on Supernatural Powers" or the "Chapter on Spiritual Powers," is the third chapter of the Yoga Sutras of Patanjali and contains 55 sutras.

The initial sutras from 1 to 15 describe the complexity of the internal process of Ashtanga Yoga covered by Dharna, Dhyan and Samadhi.

The ability to practice three higher stages of yoga Dharna (Concentration), Dhyan (Meditation) and Samadhi (State of ecstatic union), in a smooth flow without a break, is given a separate name called 'Samyama' (Complete Control or Restrain of inner faculty.

In Samyama the yogi effortlessly progresses from the sixth stage (Dharna) directly into the seventh (Dhyan) and from seventh into the eighth (Samadhi); the final stage.

An example of an oil stream is given to provide an image of no interruption. In the state of Samyama, Dhyan is likened to the steady flame of a lamp in a room devoid of any breeze.

An accomplished yogi having acquired Samyama becomes deeply aware of the realm of mind and emotions. He begins to recognise where thoughts, ideas, images and memories arise.

By regular practice of the sequential three higher stages, one gains mastery over the mental and emotional urges, and then the illuminating insight becomes available for usage.

The mind energy and emotional feelings periodically assume a stillness (blankness) wherein there is no activity of their own accord.

This happens just after an idea or image subsides, and just before another one begins.

A seeker needs to focus on this blank interval and consciously try to extend this no activity period by ignoring the next stream of thoughts emerging in the background.

Two factors help a seeker immensely; continuous and long practice and deepening of Vairagya

(Detachment) from worldly activities.

Practice has the same role as in learning Cycling and Swimming. It helps us get the required poise or flow.

Detachment from worldly activities helps reduce the endless stream of thoughts or images. Both seem to work in tandem towards achieve unwavering and firm Meditation (Dhyan).

Sutras 16 to 55 describe the attainment of various spiritual powers or Siddhis that can arise as a result of dedicated yoga practice.

An overview of the various aspects of these Siddhis or Vibhutis (Special Attributes or Abilities) covered in the Vibhuti Pada is given below:

Introduction to Vibhutis (Sutras 16-19):
-The Vibhuti Pada begins by introducing the concept of vibhutis, which are supernatural powers or extraordinary abilities that can manifest through the practice of yoga.

- It states that these Vibhutis arise from birth, the use of herbs, mantras, austerities, or through the concentration of the mind (samadhi).

Means of Attaining Vibhutis (Sutras 20-37):

- This section outlines various practices and techniques that can lead to the attainment of vibhutis.

- It discusses practices such as cultivating friendliness, compassion, joy, and equanimity towards all beings (sutras 23-24).

- It also mentions practices like regulation of the breath (pranayama), focusing the mind on various objects, and contemplating the nature of the self (sutras 25-34).

Specific Vibhutis (Sutras 38-45):

- The Vibhuti Pada describes several specific vibhutis or supernatural abilities that can be attained through yoga practice.

- These include the ability to become as small as an atom (animan), to become infinitely large (mahiman), to become infinitely heavy (gariman), and to acquire complete mastery over the elements (prakamya).

- Other vibhutis mentioned include the ability to levitate (laghiman), control the senses (indriya-jayah), and obtain knowledge of the past and future (purvajatijnanam).

The Limitations of Vibhutis (Sutras 46-49):

- While acknowledging the attainment of vibhutis, the Vibhuti Pada also warns against becoming attached to or distracted by these powers.

- It emphasises that these abilities are merely by-products of yoga practice and should not be the primary goal.

- The ultimate aim of yoga is the cessation of the fluctuations of the mind (chitta-vritti-nirodha) and the attainment of liberation (kaivalya).

The Seed of Omniscience (Sutras 50-51):

-These sutras introduce the concept of the "seed of omniscience" (sarvajnabijakam), which is the potential for complete knowledge and understanding.

- This seed is said to be present in those who have discriminated between the pure consciousness (Purusha) and the material world (Prakriti).

The Attainment of Kaivalya (Sutras 52-55):

- The Vibhuti Pada concludes by discussing the attainment of kaivalya, which is the ultimate goal of yoga practice.

- Kaivalya is the state of complete freedom, where the individual consciousness (Purusha) is liberated from the bondage of matter (Prakriti) and all afflictions (kleshas).

- The final sutras suggest that kaivalya can be attained through the renunciation of even the desire for vibhutis and the cultivation of discriminative discernment (viveka-khyati).

Thus the Vibhuti Pada of the Yoga Sutras explores the concept of supernatural powers or vibhutis that can arise as a result of dedicated yoga practice. However, it also emphasises that these abilities should not be the primary goal and that the ultimate aim of yoga is the attainment of liberation (kaivalya) through the cessation of mental fluctuations and the realisation of the true nature of consciousness.

Below is an elaboration on some of the key attributes mentioned and the warnings against their misuse as available in related literature:

1. Physical Abilities:

- Animan (the ability to become infinitesimally small)
- Mahiman (the ability to become infinitely large)
- Gariman (the ability to become infinitely heavy)
- Laghiman (the ability to levitate or become weightless)

Caution: These physical abilities, while remarkable, are not the ultimate goal of yoga practice. Attachment to or misuse of these powers can lead to egotism, distraction from the path of liberation, and potentially harmful consequences.

2. Mastery over Elements and Nature:

- Prakamya (the ability to have complete mastery over the elements of nature)

- Control over natural phenomena, such as rain, fire, and storms

Caution: While these abilities may seem impressive, they should not be used for personal gain, manipulation, or harm to others or the environment. Misuse of such powers goes against the principles of non-violence (ahimsa) and ethical conduct (yamas and niyamas) in yoga.

3. Extrasensory Perception and Knowledge:

- Clairvoyance (the ability to perceive things beyond the normal range of senses)

- Knowledge of past and future lives (purvajatijnanam)

- Omniscience (sarvajnabijakam, the seed of complete knowledge)

Caution: These abilities should not be used for selfish purposes or to violate the privacy of others. They should be approached with humility, compassion, and a commitment to using the knowledge for the greater good.

4. Control over the Mind and Senses:

- Indriya-jayah (control over the senses)

- Mastery over the mind and its modifications

Caution: While control over the mind and senses is essential for spiritual growth, it should not be used to manipulate or exploit others. The ultimate goal is the purification of the mind and the attainment of liberation, not the subjugation of others.

Essentially, the Vibhuti Pada acknowledges the existence of extraordinary abilities but emphasises the importance of using them ethically, with restraint, and without attachment, always keeping the ultimate goal of self-realization and liberation in mind.

NINE

A LIBERATED YOGI - KAIVALYA PADA

Om Shanti

After earlier chapters providing focus on Sadhna, Samadhi and Vibhuti Padas, we attempt to get a context of the to this concluding chapter of the Patanjali Yoga Sutra in three initial sutras reproduced below:

I.2 yogaa citta-vetti-nirodhai

Yoga is to still the patterning of consciousness.

I.3 tada draæui svarupe vasthanam

Then, pure awareness can abide in its very nature.

I.4 vetti-sarupyam itaratra

Otherwise, awareness takes itself to be the patterns of consciousness.

The ultimate goal of the Yoga or Samadhi is not to still (quieten) the perturbation of consciousness (Chitta) as indicated in sutra I.2 but to abide in our true nature as emphasised by the sutra I.3. If this is not achieved, the awareness returns to the patterns of consciousness as clearly stated in Sutra I.4 above.

The ultimate goal of abiding in our true nature is named state of Kaivalya. Kaivalya literally means "isolation", but as used in the Sutras, stands for emancipation, liberation and used interchangeably with moksha (liberation), which is the goal of Yoga.

The Kaivalya Pada consisting of 34 sutras, describes the nature of liberation and the reality of the transcendental self. It presents the possibilities for a person with a highly refined mind, when the mind becomes the servant and not the master.

It focuses on what happens when you take control of your thoughts rather than having your thoughts control you.

The Sutras not only provide yoga with a thorough and consistent philosophical basis, they also clarify many important esoteric concepts which are common to all traditions of Indian thought, such as karma.

The Kaivalya Pada, also known as the "Book on Absolute Freedom, delves into the ultimate goal of yoga practice – the attainment of kaivalya, or complete liberation from the cycle of birth and death.

This chapter is also a summary of the previous three chapters with a nuanced view of the practice of yoga. Following paragraphs provide key point deliberated upon.

1. The Nature of Kaivalya :

- Kaivalya is defined as the state of aloneness or isolation of the pure consciousness (purusha) from the material world (prakriti).

- It is the separation of the seer (the pure consciousness) from the seen (the objects of perception).

- The attainment of kaivalya is the ultimate aim of yoga, as it leads to the cessation of all afflictions (kleshas) and the ending of suffering.

2. The Means to Kaivalya :

- The Kaivalya Pada outlines various practices and means to achieve the state of kaivalya.

- It emphasizes the importance of cultivating discriminative discernment (viveka-khyati) to distinguish between the pure consciousness and the material world.

- Practices such as meditation (dhyana), contemplation (samadhi), and the cultivation of virtues like non-attachment (aparigraha) and contentment (santosha) are prescribed.

3. The Obstacles to Kaivalya :

- This section identifies and discusses the obstacles that can hinder the attainment of kaivalya.

- These include afflictions (kleshas) such as ignorance (avidya), egotism (asmita), attachment (raga), aversion (dvesha), and the fear of death or clinging to life (abhinivesha).

- It also mentions other obstacles like doubts, negligence, carelessness, and a lack of perseverance in yoga practice.

4. The Stages of Samadhi :

- The Kaivalya Pada describes different stages of samadhi, or meditative absorption, that lead to the realization of the true nature of consciousness.

- These stages include samprajnata samadhi (with an object of meditation) and asamprajnata samadhi (without an object of meditation).

- The final stage, nirbija samadhi, is the state of seedless or objectless samadhi, which leads to the ultimate liberation of kaivalya.

5. The Transformation of the Mind :

- This section explores the transformation of the mind (chitta) through the practice of yoga.

- It discusses the various modifications of the mind, such as the gross (vitarka), the subtle (vichara), and the blissful (ananda).

- The sutra describes the process of purifying the mind and attaining a state of one-pointedness (ekagrata), which is essential for samadhi and kaivalya.

6. The Attainment of Kaivalya :

- The final portion of the Kaivalya Pada delves into the culmination of yoga practice – the attainment of kaivalya.

- It describes the state of kaivalya as the complete cessation of the modifications of the mind and the realization of the pure consciousness (purusha).

- This section also touches upon the concept of the Enlightened Ones (Siddhas), who have attained kaivalya and are free from the cycle of birth and death.

Throughout the Kaivalya Pada, Patanjali emphasizes the importance of cultivating virtues such as non-attachment, contentment, and ethical conduct (yamas and niyamas) as essential prerequisites for attaining kaivalya.

The path to liberation is described as a gradual process of purifying the mind, overcoming afflictions, and realizing the true nature of consciousness.

The Kaivalya Pada serves as a culmination of the Yoga Sutras, providing a comprehensive guide to the ultimate goal of yoga practice – the attainment of absolute freedom (kaivalya) from the bondage of the material world and the cycle of rebirth.

Some key practical recommendations based on the teachings of the Kaivalya Pada are enumerated below:

1. Cultivate Discriminative Discernment (Viveka-Khyati):

- Develop the ability to discriminate between the eternal, pure consciousness (Purusha) and the ever-changing material world (Prakriti).

- This discernment is crucial for detaching from the illusion of identifying with the body, mind, and ego, and realizing one's true nature as the witness consciousness.

2. Practice Meditation (Dhyana) and Contemplation (Samadhi):

- Engage in regular meditation practice to calm the fluctuations of the mind (chitta-vritti).

- Progress through the stages of meditation, from samprajnata samadhi (with an object of meditation) to asamprajnata samadhi (without an object), and ultimately aim for nirbija samadhi (seedless samadhi), which leads to kaivalya.

3. Develop One-Pointedness of Mind (Ekagrata):

- Through consistent practice, cultivate the ability to focus the mind on a single point of concentration without wavering.

- This one-pointedness (ekagrata) is essential for attaining the deepest states of meditation and realizing the true nature of consciousness.

4. Embrace the Yamas and Niyamas:

- Adhere to the ethical principles outlined in the Yoga Sutras, such as non-violence (ahimsa), truthfulness (satya), non-stealing (asteya), continence (brahmacharya), and non-possessiveness (aparigraha).

- Cultivate the personal observances (niyamas) of purity (shaucha), contentment (santosha), austerity (tapas), self-study (svadhyaya), and devotion to the Lord (Ishvara-pranidhana).

- These moral and ethical practices purify the mind and create a solid foundation for spiritual growth.

5. Overcome the Kleshas (Afflictions):

- Identify and work on overcoming the five afflictions (kleshas) – ignorance (avidya), egoism (asmita), attachment (raga), aversion (dvesha), and clinging to life (abhinivesha).

- Develop non-attachment (vairagya) and cultivate virtues like contentment (santosha) to overcome these afflictions, which are obstacles to kaivalya.

6. Embrace Perseverance and Consistency:

- Understand that the path to kaivalya is a gradual process that requires unwavering perseverance and consistency in practice.

- Develop the determination to overcome obstacles, such as doubts, negligence, and carelessness, which can hinder progress on the spiritual journey.

7. Seek Guidance and Knowledge:

- Study the teachings of the Yoga Sutras and other sacred texts under the guidance of a qualified teacher or guru.

- Embrace the teachings with an open mind, and be willing to question and contemplate their deeper meanings.

- Cultivate the virtue of self-study (svadhyaya) to deepen your understanding and progress on the path.

By following above practical suggestions from the Kaivalya Pada, a seeker can gradually purify the mind, overcome the afflictions, and progress towards the ultimate goal of kaivalya – the complete liberation of consciousness from the bondage of the material world and the cycle of birth and death.

Having described the general situation of our life and a practical approach to seek our true self by techniques prescribed by Patanjali yoga Sutras in previous chapters, it is time to plan a way forward.

One very important aspect of this journey is reading or listening to Scriptures to get the necessary information which may help us in developing the detachment (Vairagya) and discrimination (Vivek) while living our daily life.

Regular practice of the eight limbs of Yoga as described by Patanjali along with the regular intake of Scriptures (Shravan) followed by reflection (Manan) on those concepts helps us greatly in Meditation (Nididhyasana) ; the three pillars of Vedantic study leading to Samadhi state.

To begin with we plan to focus on explanatory texts (Prakarana Granthas) that do an excellent job of introducing and explaining Vedanta systematically and thus help us grasp nuanced knowledge available through Prasthana Trayi (Triple Cannon) namely Upanishads, Brahma Sutras and Bhagwat Gita.

From the next chapter onward we begin with Tattva Bodha followed by Vivek Chudamani and Atma Bodha. These texts by Adi Shankaracharya are very helpful in providing us necessary grounding to be able to follow the knowledge disseminated in Upanishads , Bhagwat Gita and Brahma Sutras, if taken up by the reader.

We have, however, included brief introduction to Prasthana Trayi (Triple Cannon) namely Upanishads, Brahma Sutras and Bhagwat Gita in three Appendices (A to C) placed at the end of this book. Reader may learn in depth, about these important texts by referring to some good commentries on them. Bibliography section may help in identification of such resources.

TEN
THE AWAKENING TO REALITY - TATTVA BODHA

Hari Om

In previous chapters we have attempted an overview of the Spirituality discipline. We have also got a nodding acquaintance with the Patanjali Yoga sutras, that propose a practical approach for a seeker on the path of Spirituality.

One important aspect of preparatory phase is self study (Svadhyaya) of scriptures as it helps the seeker understand the context and strengthens Vairagya(detachment/ dispassion) and Vivek (discernment/discrimination) ; the two key ingredients that are crucial for meaningful progress in this discipline.

As indicated in previous chapter 9, we begin with Tattva Bodha, written by Adi Shankaracharya, a comprehensive text that covers a wide range of topics related to Advaita Vedanta philosophy.

Following main topics are covered in this work

1. Introduction to Brahman:

- Definition and nature of Brahman (the ultimate reality)

- Attributes of Brahman (existence, consciousness, and bliss)

- Brahman as the cause of the universe

2. The Nature of the Self (Atman):
- Distinction between the Self and the body, mind, and senses
- The Self as the knower, the subject of knowledge
- The Self as the witness consciousness

3. The Identity of Brahman and the Self:
- The doctrine of non-duality (Advaita)
- The identity of the individual Self (Jivatman) with the Supreme Self (Paramatman)
- The concept of "Tat Tvam Asi" (That Thou Art)

4. The Ignorance (Avidya) and Its Effects:
- Avidya as the root cause of bondage and suffering
- The concept of Maya (the world as an appearance)
- The effects of Avidya (creation, sustenance, and dissolution of the universe)

5. The Path to Self-Realization:
- The means of knowledge (Jnana Yoga)
- The importance of discrimination (Viveka)
- The practice of dispassion (Vairagya)

6. The Study of the Scriptures:
- The role of the Vedas, Upanishads, and other sacred texts
- The importance of a qualified teacher (Guru)
- The process of self-inquiry (Atma Vichara)

7. The Four-fold Means of Knowledge:
- Discrimination between the real and the unreal (Nitya-Anitya Vastu Viveka)
- Renunciation of the fruits of action (Iha-Amutra Phala Bhoga Viraga)
- The six virtues (Shama, Dama, Uparati, Titiksha, Samadhi, and Shraddha)
- The desire for liberation (Mumukshutva)

8. The Stages of Self-Realization:
- The preparatory stage (Shravana)
- The stage of reflection (Manana)
- The stage of direct realization (Nididhyasana)

9. The State of Liberation (Moksha):

- The nature of liberation

- The characteristics of a liberated being (Jivanmukta)

- The attainment of bliss and freedom from the cycle of birth and death

We elaborate a bit on the covered topics and place comments by few well known exponents of Spirituality in succeeding paragraphs.

1. Introduction to Brahman:

- **Definition and nature of Brahman:** Brahman is defined as the ultimate reality, the ground of all existence, and the source from which everything emanates. It is described as infinite, eternal, and indivisible, without any attributes or qualities.

- **Comment by Swami Vivekananda:** "Brahman is the infinite, the bottomless, the source less source of all manifestations in this universe."

- **Attributes of Brahman:** Existence, consciousness, and bliss (Sat-Chit-Ananda) are considered the essential attributes of Brahman.

- **Comment by Dr. Radhakrishnan:** "The highest reality is not merely Being, but Being-Consciousness-Bliss (Satchidananda)."

- **Brahman as the cause of the universe:** Brahman is presented as the efficient and material cause of the universe, from which the entire cosmos manifests.

- **Comment by Swami Chinmayananda:** "Brahman is both the cause and the effect, the material and the instrumental cause of this universe."

2. The Nature of the Self (Atman):

- Distinction between the Self and the body, mind, and senses: Tattva Bodha emphasizes the distinction between the Self (Atman) and the physical body, the mind, and the senses, which are considered as instruments or vehicles of experience.

- **Comment by Swami Nikhilananda:** "The Self is not the body, not the senses, not the mind, nor even the intellect. It is the witness of all these."

- **The Self as the knower and the subject of knowledge:** The Self is presented as the eternal, conscious principle that is the knower and the subject of all knowledge.

- **Comment by Swami Sivananda:** "The Self is the seer, the witness, the knower, and the subject of all experiences."

- The Self as the witness consciousness: The Self is described as the witness consciousness that remains unaffected by the activities of the mind, body, and senses.

- Comment by Swami Dayananda Saraswati: "The Self is the witness consciousness, the pure awareness that illumines all experiences."

3. The Identity of Brahman and the Self:

- **The doctrine of non-duality (Advaita):** Tattva Bodha expounds the central principle of Advaita Vedanta, which is the non-duality or the unity of Brahman and the Self.

- **Comment by Sri Aurobindo:** "Advaita is the supreme spiritual experience, the realisation of the identity of the individual self with the universal Self."

- **The identity of the individual Self (Jivatman) with the Supreme Self (Paramatman):** The text establishes the identity of the individual Self (Jivatman) with the Supreme Self (Paramatman), which is Brahman.

- **Comment by Swami Krishnananda:** "The individual self and the universal Self are not two different entities, but one and the same Reality."

- **The concept of "Tat Tvam Asi" (That Thou Art):** The famous Upanishadic statement "Tat Tvam Asi" (That Thou Art) is discussed, which affirms the identity of the individual Self with the Supreme Self.

- **Comment by Swami Vivekananda:** "The whole universe is that Brahman, existing from eternity to eternity. That is the teaching of the Upanishads."

4. The Ignorance (Avidya) and Its Effects:

- **Avidya as the root cause of bondage and suffering:** Tattva Bodha explains that Avidya, or ignorance of the true nature of the Self, is the root cause of bondage, suffering, and the cycle of birth and death.

- Comment by Swami Sivananda: "Ignorance is the cause of all miseries and bondage. Knowledge of the Self alone can remove this ignorance."

- **The concept of Maya**: Maya, often translated as illusion or appearance, is discussed as the projective power of Brahman that creates the appearance of the phenomenal world.

- **Comment by Sri Aurobindo**: "Maya is the self-projection of the infinite for self-manifestation in the dynamism of the finite."

- **The effects of Avidya**: The text elaborates on the effects of Avidya, which include the creation, sustenance, and dissolution of the universe, as well as the individual's identification with the body, mind, and senses.

- **Comment by Swami Chinmayananda**: "Avidya is the cause of the individual's identification with the body, mind, and senses, leading to the cycle of birth and death."

5. The Path to Self-Realization:

- The means of knowledge (Jnana Yoga): Tattva Bodha emphasizes the importance of Jnana Yoga, or the path of knowledge, as the primary means to attain self-realization.

- **Comment by Swami Vivekananda**: "Jnana Yoga is the realization of the Self through study, reflection, and meditation on the sacred texts."

- **The importance of discrimination (Viveka)**: The text stresses the necessity of developing Viveka, which is the ability to discriminate between the real and the unreal, the permanent and the impermanent.

- **Comment by Swami Nikhilananda**: "Viveka is the power of discrimination between the eternal and the non-eternal, the real and the unreal."

- **The practice of dispassion (Vairagya)**: Vairagya, or dispassion towards the objects of the world, is presented as an essential quality for self-realization.

- **Comment by Swami Sivananda**: "Vairagya is the renunciation of desires and the cultivation of indifference towards worldly objects."

6. The Study of the Scriptures:

- **The role of the Vedas, Upanishads, and other sacred texts:** Tattva Bodha highlights the importance of studying the Vedas, Upanishads, and other sacred texts as sources of knowledge for self-realization.

- **Comment by Swami Dayananda Saraswati:** "The Upanishads are the most authoritative sources of knowledge for understanding the nature of the Self."

- **The importance of a qualified teacher (Guru):** The text emphasizes the need for a qualified teacher or Guru to guide the student in understanding the scriptures and imparting the knowledge of the Self.

- **Comment by Swami Chinmayananda:** "The Guru is the embodiment of the teachings and plays a vital role in removing the doubts and misconceptions of the student."

- **The process of self-inquiry (Atma Vichara):** Self-inquiry, or Atma Vichara, is presented as a method of self-analysis and self-examination to understand the true nature of the Self.

- **Comment by Ramana Maharshi:** "The inquiry 'Who am I?' is the principal means of attaining self-knowledge."

7. The Four-fold Means of Knowledge:

- **Discrimination between the real and the unreal (Nitya-Anitya Vastu Viveka):** This aspect involves developing the ability to discriminate between the eternal and the non-eternal, the real and the unreal.

- **Comment by Swami Sivananda:** "Nitya-Anitya Vastu Viveka is the discrimination between the eternal and the non-eternal, the Self and the non-Self."

- **Renunciation of the fruits of action (Iha-Amutra Phala Bhoga Viraga):** This refers to the detachment from the desire for the results of one's actions, both in this life and the next.

- **Comment by Swami Vivekananda:** "Renunciation means giving up all attachment to the fruits of work."

- **The six virtues (Shama, Dama, Uparati, Titiksha, Samadhi, and Shraddha):** Tattva Bodha discusses the six virtues or qualities that are essential for self-realization, including control of the mind and senses, patience, concentration, and faith.

- **Comment by Swami Nikhilananda:** "These six virtues are the prerequisites for the attainment of self-knowledge."

- **The desire for liberation (Mumukshutva):** The text emphasizes the importance of developing an intense desire for liberation or Moksha, which is the ultimate goal of the spiritual seeker.

Adi Shankaracharya's teachings in Tattva Bodha can possibly be implemented in our daily lives in the following ways:

1. Understanding the nature of Brahman:

Tattva Bodha begins by establishing the nature of Brahman, the absolute reality that pervades all existence. Brahman is described as the ultimate truth, infinite, eternal, and indivisible.

To apply this teaching, one can cultivate a sense of reverence and awe for the divine essence present in all beings and aspects of life. This realization can foster a deeper appreciation for the interconnectedness of all things and promote a mindset of unity and harmony.

2. Recognizing the Self (Atman):

Tattva Bodha emphasizes the understanding of the Self (Atman) as being distinct from the body, mind, and senses. The Self is portrayed as the eternal, conscious principle within each individual.

In daily life, this teaching can help us detach from our identification with the physical and mental aspects of our existence. By recognizing the Self as the true essence, we can develop a sense of inner peace and equanimity, even amidst the ups and downs of life.

3. Overcoming ignorance (Avidya):

Avidya, or ignorance, is considered the root cause of suffering and bondage in Advaita Vedanta. Tattva Bodha aims to dispel this ignorance by providing the knowledge of the Self and its relationship with Brahman.

In practical terms, we can overcome ignorance by cultivating self-awareness, engaging in self-inquiry, and constantly questioning our limiting beliefs and conditioned patterns of thought and behavior.

4. Practicing discrimination (Viveka):

Tattva Bodha emphasizes the importance of discrimination, or viveka, to distinguish between the real and the unreal, the permanent and the impermanent.

In daily life, this teaching can be applied by developing the ability to discern between the essential and the non-essential, prioritizing our actions and thoughts based on what truly matters, and letting go of attachments to transient experiences and possessions.

5. Cultivating dispassion (Vairagya):

Dispassion, or vairagya, is the state of freedom from desires and cravings. Tattva Bodha encourages the development of vairagya as a means to liberate oneself from the cycle of birth and death.

In practical terms, we can cultivate dispassion by practicing contentment, moderation, and mindfulness in our daily lives. By reducing our attachment to material possessions and external sources of happiness, we can experience a greater sense of inner freedom and peace.

6. Practicing meditation and contemplation:

Tattva Bodha emphasizes the importance of meditation and contemplation as means to attain self-realization.

In daily life, we can incorporate these practices by setting aside dedicated time for introspection, silent reflection, and the exploration of our inner selves. Regular meditation can help calm the mind, cultivate awareness, and deepen our understanding of the teachings of Advaita Vedanta.

By incorporating these teachings into our daily lives, we can gradually develop a deeper understanding of the ultimate reality and our true nature, leading to a state of inner peace, wisdom, and liberation.

ELEVEN

OUR SPIRITUAL COMPASS - VIVEK CHUDAMANI BY ADI SHANKARACHARYA

Hari Om

Brahman alone is real, the universe is unreal and the individual soul is no other than the Universal Soul.

- Vivek Chudamani

It is told that when Swami Vivekanand first met his spiritual Guru Shri Ramakrishna, he, then known as Narendra, enquired if his future Guru had seen God.

Saint's reply was in affirmative and he emphasized that he sees God more clearly than he is able to see Narendra.This exchange between the two is key to our understanding the world around us.

Our waking experience is intuitively considered more real than a dream, as the persistence of our waking world is more than that of a dream.

After the dream is over we land in our waking reality which seems to have a continuity.

However, on closer examination we may realize that our waking world is also continuously changing. Our bodies age, our parents die and the politico-social situation of the world is in a continuous flux.

The ability to discriminate between Real and Unreal (Sat and Asat) is the key attribute necessary for a spiritual seeker.

All assertions about our true nature would fall on deaf ears till we really understand reality.The Vedic prayer to God about taking us to 'Sat' from 'Asat' is in the same spirit.

In the previous chapter 10, we had attempted some understanding of Tattva Bodha by Adi Shankaracharya which emphasized the key facts about the world around us and reality within us.

Continuing In the same direction, we peruse, Vivek Chudamani, a Sanskrit philosophical text written by Adi Shankaracharya, to strengthen our discrimination (Vivek) ability.

It is important to understand that our problems emanate from ignorance and it can be removed by right knowledge only.

One may use any of the available paths like Bhakti, Karma or Jnana to achieve the required knowledge or insight essential for overcoming darkness of Avidya (Ignorance).

Our Vedic prayer to lead us to light from darkness underlines this eternal urge within us.

This text of Vivek Chudamani, in a very systematic way, provides us illumination to remove our ignorance. Repetitive reading and contemplation is the only way to achieve our objective.

Shankaracharya is one of the most influential thinkers and spiritual leaders of Advaita Vedanta, the non-dualistic school of Hindu philosophy.

The Vivek Chudamani is divided into several sections, each dealing with a specific aspect of Advaita Vedanta philosophy and the path to self-realization.

1. Introduction:

The text begins with an introduction that sets the stage for the dialogue between the teacher (Guru) and the disciple (Shishya). It emphasizes the importance of discriminating between the real and the unreal, which is the essence of the text.

2. The Qualifications for Self-Realization:

This section discusses the four essential qualifications (Sadhana Chatushtaya) required for attaining self-realization:

a) Discrimination between the real and the unreal (Nitya-Anitya Vastu Viveka)

b) Renunciation (Vairagya)

c) The six virtues (Shatsampat)- Tranquility (Shama), Self-control (Dama), Renunciation (Uparati), Forbearance (Titiksha), Faith (Shraddha), and Concentration (Samadhana) are the six virtues, the six treasures that one have to cultivate.

d) Intense desire for liberation (Mumukshutva).

3. The Nature of the Self:

Here, Shankaracharya explains the true nature of the Self (Atman) as distinct from the body, mind, and intellect. The Self is described as an eternal, pure consciousness, and the ultimate reality (Brahman).

4. The Path to Self-Realization:

This section outlines the various paths or means (Sadhanās) to attain self-realization, such as study of the scriptures (Sravana), contemplation (Manana), and meditation (Nididhyasana). It also discusses the obstacles (Vikshepa) that hinder progress on the path and how to overcome them.

5. The Attainment of Self-Realization:

This part describes the state of self-realization (Jivanmukti) and the experience of the highest bliss (Ananda) that results from the realization of one's true nature as the Self.

6. The Means and Stages of Self-Realization:

Here, Shankaracharya elaborates on the different stages and means of self-realization, such as the practice of discrimination (Viveka), detachment (Vairagya), control of the mind (Sama), and concentration (Dama).

7. The Liberated State:

The final section discusses the state of complete liberation (Videhamukti) and the dissolution of individual existence into the ultimate reality (Brahman).

Some suggestions for implementing the teachings of Vivek Chudamani in daily life are given below.

1. **Cultivate discrimination (Viveka):** Develop the ability to distinguish between the permanent and the impermanent, the real and the unreal, the Self and the non-Self. This helps to shift the focus from the external to the internal.

2. **Practice detachment (Vairagya):** Gradually develop dispassion towards worldly objects and desires, recognizing their transient nature. This promotes inner peace and equanimity.

3. **Develop virtues (Shat Sampat):** Cultivate the six virtues prescribed in the text, such as tranquility (Shama), self-control (Dama), renunciation (Uparati), forbearance (Titiksha), faith (Shraddha), and concentration (Samadhana).

4. **Study the scriptures (Sravana):** Regularly study and contemplate on the teachings of Advaita Vedanta and other spiritual texts to gain a deeper understanding of the Self and the path to self-realization.

5. **Practice meditation (Nididhyasana):** Engage in regular meditation practices to calm the mind, develop concentration, and gain direct experience of the Self.

6. **Serve selflessly (Karma Yoga):** Perform actions with detachment and without expectation of reward, recognizing that the true Self is the witness of all actions.

7. **Cultivate devotion (Bhakti):** Develop devotion and surrender to the Supreme Reality, recognizing that the Self and Brahman are one and the same.

By incorporating the above suggestions into daily life, one can gradually purify the mind, overcome delusion, and progress towards the ultimate goal of self-realization and liberation.

Vivek Chudamani, being a seminal work of Adi Shankaracharya, has been widely acclaimed and commented upon by various exponents and scholars within the domain of spirituality and Advaita Vedanta philosophy. Here are some notable comments and observations made by prominent figures:

1. Swami Vivekananda, the famous 19th-century Hindu monk and philosopher, highly regarded Vivek Chudamani. He described it as "one of the most perfect works in Sanskrit literature for practicality and eloquence."

2. **Sri Ramana Maharshi**, the renowned Indian sage and exponent of Advaita Vedanta, often recommended the study of Vivek Chudamani to his disciples. He praised the text for its clarity and depth in expounding the principles of non-dualism.

3. **Swami Chinmayananda**, a prominent 20th-century Hindu spiritual leader and teacher, wrote an extensive commentary on Vivek Chudamani. He regarded the text as "a masterpiece of spiritual literature" and praised its ability to guide seekers on the path of self-realization.

4. **Swami Sivananda**, the founder of the Divine Life Society, described Vivek Chudamani as "a brilliant and illuminating work" that encapsulates the essence of Advaita Vedanta philosophy in a concise and lucid manner.

5. Sri Nisargadatta Maharaj, a renowned Advaita teacher and spiritual master, often referred to Vivek Chudamani in his teachings and conversations. He acknowledged the text's profound insights into the nature of the Self and the path to self-realization.

6. **Sri Chandrashekhara Bharati Mahaswamigal,** a prominent 20th-century Advaita scholar and the 34th Jagadguru of Sringeri Sharada Peetham, wrote a detailed commentary on Vivek Chudamani, titled "Vivekachudamani Vyakhya." He praised the text for its clarity and depth in elucidating the principles of non-dualism.

7. **Swami Satchidanandendra Saraswati,** a renowned Advaita scholar and the current Jagadguru of Kamakoti Peetham, has written extensively on Vivek Chudamani and its importance in understanding Shankaracharya's teachings.

These comments from esteemed spiritual leaders and scholars highlight the profound impact and significance of Vivek Chudamani within the Advaita Vedanta tradition. The text continues to be widely studied and revered as a concise yet comprehensive guide to the principles of non-dualism and the path to self-realization.

The video resources shared in the online section are highly recommended and provide a very nuanced understanding of abstract ideas with real world examples.

TWELVE

WHO AM I ? -ATMA BODHA (KNOWLEDGE OF SELF)

Hari Om

Tapobhih Ksheenapaapaanaam Santanaam Veetaraginaam
Mumukshoonaam
Apekshyoyam Atmabodho Vidheeyate
(This Atma Bodha is designed for the benefit of those who got
rid of sins by doing penance,
those who have a peaceful mind, those who could overcome
their cravings,
and those who are desirous of moksha or liberation.)

- First Verse of Atma Bodha

The very first verse of Atma Bodh, consisting of 68 verses, describes the qualification of the target audience who may benefit from the truth being revealed.

In last chapter 11 on Vivek Chudamani, we had described amongst other things, the six virtues (Shat Sampat)- Tranquility (Shama), Self-control (Dama), Renunciation (Uparati), Forbearance

(Titiksha), Faith (Shraddha), and Concentration (Samadhana) as essential for a seeker on path of self knowledge.

These six virtues seem to map well with the qualification suggested in the first verse of Atma Bodha.

There is some pragmatic logic to these virtues that a seeker may try to acquire. It is not essential to be born with these virtues, but over time, sincere efforts may be made to cultivate them.

If we pause and reflect, the same virtues are essential for success in any worldly field also, only context may change.

If the goal is material wealth, the renunciation of complacency and a faith in efficacy of material wealth, may be the essential virtues.

Other virtues like Tranquility, Self-Control, Forbearance and Concentration are required in good measures, even if one wants to succeed in the material world.

Scientific discoveries and technical innovations may be difficult if one is not able to manifest these six virtues in good measure.

A seeker of 'spirituality-within' only changes his focus from external to internal world.

After visiting our inner world and gaining a glimpse of our true self, a transformation seems to occur in our personality which ensures that we are better adapted, psychologically, to the ups and downs of life in the external world also.

If we see the life of great masters, we notice a consistent pattern of being useful to society at large while maintaining a pleasant disposition.

So, if majority of us get a glimpse of the true self and modify our behaviour in dealing with our fellow beings, world may become a better place to live.

However, this is only a virtuous offshoot of mass Spirituality. A true seeker is not really affected by the ongoing socio-political events and continues to be useful to society with an equanimity of disposition.

The key message for the beginners on this path is that half-hearted measures may not help us. Dedicated commitment is necessary for seekers of Spirituality.

If for some reason, we are comfortable with mixed offerings of life and the existential questions; like 'why we are here' and 'what is the ultimate purpose of it all', do not bother us, we would be better off keeping out of it till we are ripe to undertake this journey.

This refrain is not to discourage seekers from exploring it but to ensure a better chance of progress in the chosen path. The seeker may slowly but surely cultivate the required foundational attributes. Patanjali's Sadhna pada also underscores similar qualities in a seeker.

Having set the context, let us explore what Atma Bodh has for us. After all, it is talking about aspects of us that for various reasons we are not aware of.

As we acquire knowledge of our latest gadgets (Mobile, Laptop, Car), why not learn about our own self?

This journey of listening to the videos in the resource section and reading the key aspects of ourselves in Atma Bodha text, is certainly not going to hurt us.

Life is a long and iterative process. Though 'Truth' as revealed in Scriptures is unchanging, our understanding of it evolves over time.

First sincere step on this journey is what really sets us apart from billions of human beings who are comfortable in the status quo and accept life challenges passively. Listening may lead to mental reflection followed by behavioral change.

Atma Bodh, also known as the Knowledge of the Self, is a renowned work by the great Indian philosopher and spiritual teacher, Adi Shankaracharya (788-820 CE).

This text is considered a foundational work in the Advaita Vedanta tradition, which emphasizes the non-dual nature of reality and the ultimate oneness of the individual self (Atman) with the universal Brahman.

According to Atma Bodha, we have three distinct bodies (Sareeras) namely, Sthoola (Gross), Sookshma (Subtle) and Karana(Causal).

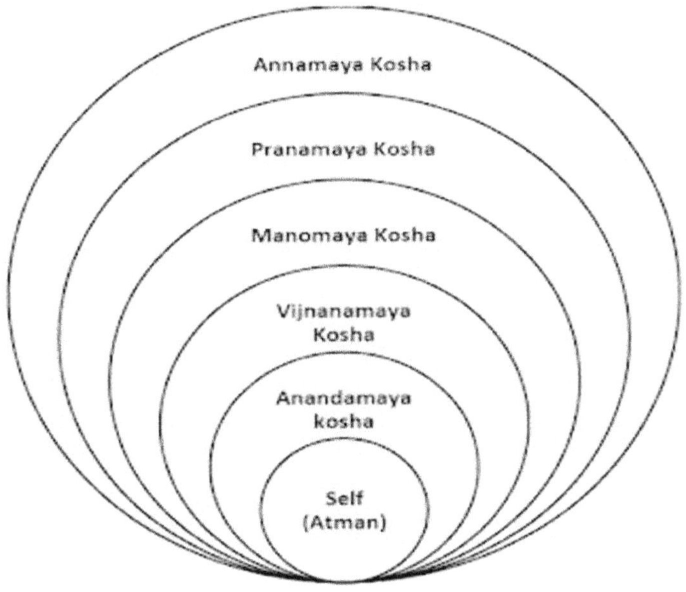

Fig 1 : The pictorial view of five Sheaths that constitute our personality

We have studied Panch Kosha Vivek in earlier chapters and our gross body is equivalent to Annamaya Kosha in that construct. **Figure 1** is reproduced from earlier chapterto refresh our memory.

Subtle body, the Sookshma Sareera, is a combination of seventeen ingredients, five pranas, ten organs (5 sense organs and 5 organs of action), mind and Intellect, the instruments with which we experience pain and pleasure. It is thus composed of three koshas namely, Pranamaya, Manomaya and Vijnanamaya koshas as indicated in **Fig.1** above.

Causal body, the Karan Sareera, is also called Avidya (Ignorance) and is the cause of both gross and subtle bodies.

Anandmaya Kosha of Panch Kosha viveka corresponds to the Causal body. Based on our past karmas and impressions stored in the Causal body we get appropriate subtle and gross body.

The Sthoola Sareera, gross body, is the one that gets old, diseased and dies. Sookshma Sareera leaves the gross body at the time of death and gets rebirth.

It is not Atma that gets rebirth, according to Advaita doctrine. Atma is nothing but a form of Paramatma, the Brahman. It manifests itself in Sookshma Sareera and gets involved in the ties of human relations and gets elations and sorrows.

It also does various Karmas both good and bad. The results of those Karmas follow and the Sookshma Sareera gets the rewards called good births and punishments called mean births.

This process of rebirth stops only if in any birth this Sookshma Sareera gets out of Maya and understands the Atma in its body and gives up all worldly attachments and starts leading a life that befits Paramatma.

Then it will join Paramatma which is called Moksha. Till it is attained this worldly pleasures and sorrows will be hunting it in every birth.

Avidya (ignorance), has no beginning and is also quite difficult to define. As indicated above, it is also called Karana Sareera (Causal Body).

So every living body has three forms of sareera viz., Sthoola (gross body), Sookshma (subtle body) and Karana (causal body).

The gross body and subtle body are products of Avidya and therefore Avidya is called the causal body.

Atma is none of these three. It is the witness to the three bodies and never gets identified with them.

Atma or self luminous consciousness, illuminates the activities of the gross and subtle bodies. It is, however, detached from all the three bodies. Because of ignorance we think and attribute all the qualities of the three Sareeras to Atma.

When covered by a blue cloth, a pure colorless crystal looks like a blue crystal. Similarly because of the union with the Five Koshas, the pure Atma appears to have borrowed their qualities upon itself.

Annamaya Kosha is the physical body.

Pranamaya Kosa is the one that has Five Pranas that breathes life into this physical body.

Manomaya Kosha is responsible for our twin feelings of happiness and sorrow. It controls our mind.

Vijnanamaya Kosha controls our intellect.

These three viz. Pranamaya, Manonaya and Vijnanamaya constitute the Sookshma Sareera (Subtle body).

The Anandamaya Kosha which belongs to our Karana Sareera and controls our emotions is, however ,not real Ananda. Real and eternal Ananda (bliss) belongs to Atma.

It is therefore stated clearly in Atma Bodha that none of the three sareeras (bodies) is Atma.

If I make a statement while awake, " I had a peaceful sleep through the night except for a brief bad dream". Who could be making this statement ? In deep sleep the mind does not exist and in dream our gross body and senses of cognition are dormant, but our mind has taken the form of the dreamer. Who is that entity that is able to witness all three states namely, waking, dream and deep sleep and thus make this statement that we are analyzing?

Atma bodha makes us question our established notions and as a consequence of the process of contemplation/reflection, faulty notions are dropped and we get a glimpse of deeper aspects connected with our experience of self.

The coverage in this chapter is just to introduce the seeker to this important text and can not replace careful reading of text under guidance of an experienced teacher. The videos in the resource section may help.

Key aspects covered in Atma Bodh:

1. The Nature of the Self (Atman):

Adi Shankara begins by establishing the existence of the Atman, the true Self, which is distinct from the physical body, the mind, and the intellect. He describes the Atman as eternal, conscious, and blissful, transcending the limitations of the material world.

2. The Illusion of Duality:

Shankara explains that the perception of duality, the separation between the individual self and the ultimate reality, is an illusion caused by ignorance (avidya). This ignorance veils the true nature of the Self and leads to the attachment to the external world and the cycle of birth and death.

3. The Path to Self-Realization:

Shankara outlines the path to self-realization, which involves the pursuit of knowledge (jnana), the practice of discrimination (viveka), and the cultivation of dispassion (vairagya). He emphasizes the importance of study, contemplation, and the guidance of a qualified teacher (guru) in attaining self-knowledge.

4. The Nature of Brahman:

Shankara elucidates the concept of Brahman, the ultimate reality that is infinite, eternal, and beyond all attributes. He establishes the non-dual relationship between the Atman and Brahman, stating that they are one and the same, a realization that leads to liberation (moksha).

Details of content:

1. Cultivating Self-Awareness:

Atma Bodha emphasizes the importance of recognizing the true nature of the Self (Atman) as distinct from the body, mind, and intellect. A seeker can cultivate self-awareness by practicing introspection, meditation, and self-inquiry. This can help develop a deeper understanding of one's true identity beyond the limitations of the physical and mental realms.

2. Practicing Discrimination (Viveka):

The text stresses the need for discrimination between the real and the unreal, the permanent and the impermanent. In daily life, a seeker can practice viveka by observing their thoughts, emotions, and attachments objectively. This can help develop detachment from temporary and transient experiences, and foster a more balanced perspective.

3. Developing Dispassion (Vairagya):

Atma Bodha emphasizes the importance of dispassion or detachment from the external world and its objects. A seeker can cultivate vairagya by consciously letting go of excessive desires, cravings, and attachments. This can lead to greater inner freedom, peace, and a more meaningful engagement with life.

4. Pursuing Self-Knowledge (Atma-jnana):

The ultimate goal of Atma Bodha is the attainment of self-knowledge or the realization of the non-dual nature of the Self and Brahman. A seeker can pursue this knowledge through consistent study, contemplation, and self-inquiry practices. This can involve reading and reflecting on spiritual texts, attending discourses, and engaging in introspective practices.

5. Seeking Guidance (Guru-Upadesha):

Atma Bodha highlights the value of a qualified teacher or guru in guiding the seeker on the path of self-realization. A seeker can seek out authentic spiritual teachers, attend satsangs (spiritual discourses), or participate in study groups to receive guidance, clarify doubts, and avoid potential pitfalls on the spiritual journey.

6. Maintaining Equanimity:

The teachings of Atma Bodha encourage the cultivation of equanimity, a balanced state of mind in the face of life's challenges and vicissitudes. A seeker can strive to maintain equanimity by developing detachment from external circumstances, practicing acceptance, and cultivating inner peace through spiritual practices.

7. Living with Integrity:

Atma Bodha emphasizes the importance of living a life of integrity, guided by ethics and moral principles. A seeker can integrate these values into their daily interactions, decision-making processes, and relationships, fostering a harmonious and virtuous way of life.

By consistently applying the learnings from Atma Bodha in their daily lives, seekers can gradually transform their perspective, cultivate inner peace and freedom, and progress on the path of self-realization and spiritual growth.

Benefits of Atma Bodh in Daily Life

Adi Shankara's Atma Bodha offers profound insights and guidance for seekers on the path of self-realization. While the text delves into the metaphysical and philosophical aspects of Advaita Vedanta, it also provides practical wisdom that can be implemented in one's daily life.

Some ways in which a seeker can apply the learnings from Atma Bodha to their daily lives are given below.

1. Understanding the Nature of the Self:

Atma Bodh's teachings on the nature of the Self can help individuals develop a deeper understanding of their true identity beyond the physical and mental aspects. This understanding can cultivate a sense of inner peace, detachment from external factors, and a more meaningful connection with one's inner being.

2. Overcoming Duality and Attachment:

By recognizing the illusory nature of duality and attachment, individuals can learn to let go of false identifications and attachments that contribute to suffering. This can lead to a more balanced and peaceful approach to life, reducing the impact of external circumstances on one's inner state.

3. Cultivating Dispassion and Discrimination:

The practice of dispassion (vairagya) and discrimination (viveka) can help individuals develop a more objective and detached perspective towards the external world. This can facilitate better decision-making, reduced emotional reactivity, and a greater sense of inner freedom.

4. Pursuing Self-Knowledge:

Atma Bodh emphasizes the importance of self-knowledge (Atma-jnana) as the ultimate goal. Individuals can incorporate practices such as study, contemplation, and self-inquiry into their daily lives, gradually unveiling the deeper layers of their existence and moving towards self-realization.

5. Seeking Guidance:

Recognizing the value of a qualified teacher (guru) in the pursuit of self-knowledge can help individuals avoid potential pitfalls and misinterpretations. Engaging with authentic spiritual teachers, attending discourses, or participating in study groups can provide valuable guidance and support on the path of self-discovery.

Overall, Atma Bodha by Adi Shankaracharya offers profound insights into the nature of the Self and the path to self-realization. By integrating its teachings into daily life, individuals can cultivate a deeper sense of inner peace, detachment, and a more profound understanding of their true nature, ultimately leading to a more fulfilling and meaningful existence.

Expert Comments on Atma BodhAdi Shankara's Atma Bodha has been widely revered and studied by various spiritual luminaries and exponents of Advaita Vedanta philosophy. Here are some notable views and commentaries on this seminal work:

1. Ramana Maharshi (1879-1950):

The renowned sage Ramana Maharshi, who is considered one of the most influential spiritual figures of the 20th century, held Atma Bodha in high regard. He often recommended it to his disciples as a concise and lucid exposition of Advaita Vedanta. Ramana Maharshi's own teachings on Self-inquiry and the pursuit of the true Self resonate deeply with the essence of Atma Bodha.

2. Swami Vivekananda (1863-1902):

Swami Vivekananda, the foremost disciple of Sri Ramakrishna Paramahamsa and a pioneering figure in the dissemination of Vedanta philosophy in the West, praised Atma Bodha as a valuable text for aspirants seeking self-realization. He commended its clarity and depth in expounding the non-dual nature of reality and the path to liberation.

3. Swami Chinmayananda (1916-1993):

Swami Chinmayananda, a renowned spiritual teacher and exponent of Advaita Vedanta, wrote an extensive commentary on Atma Bodha, titled "The Self-Realization" (1966). In his commentary, he elucidated the profound teachings of Atma Bodha with clarity and practical guidance, making it accessible to modern seekers.

4. Nisargadatta Maharaj (1897-1981):

Nisargadatta Maharaj, a revered Advaita master known for his radical and direct teachings on non-duality, often referred to Atma Bodha in his discourses. He regarded it as a valuable text that encapsulated the essence of Advaita Vedanta and encouraged his disciples to study and contemplate its teachings.

5. Sri Aurobindo (1872-1950):

While Sri Aurobindo's integral philosophy differed from the traditional Advaita Vedanta perspective, he acknowledged the value and clarity of Atma Bodha in expounding the principles of non-duality and the pursuit of self-knowledge. He regarded it as a succinct and authoritative text on the Advaita philosophy.

6. Swami Sivananda (1887-1963):

Swami Sivananda, the founder of the Divine Life Society and a prolific spiritual teacher, highly recommended the study of Atma Bodha to his disciples. He considered it a concise and powerful text that encapsulated the essential teachings of Advaita Vedanta and facilitated the realization of the ultimate truth.

These views from eminent spiritual figures and exponents of Advaita Vedanta philosophy highlight the enduring relevance and profound impact of Adi Shankara's Atma Bodha. They recognized its clarity, depth, and effectiveness in guiding seekers on the path of self-realization and attaining the ultimate goal of liberation or moksha.

THIRTEEN

SYNTHESIS OF THE KNOWLEDGE GAINED IN EARLIER CHAPTERS

Hari Om

In this chapter we make an attempt to consolidate our learning so far from the earlier chapters and and later in concluding chapter 14, we plan a way forward for the seeker in a pragmatic manner.

If we try to recall the key concepts from the three highly regarded Advaita Vedanta texts, namely; Tattva Bodha, Atma Bodha and Vivek Chudamani, an underlying key message that emerges is that the realization of our true nature as the eternal, blissful Atman (Self) that is one with Brahman (Ultimate Reality) is highest goal of human birth.

Tattva Bodha (Knowledge of Truth) by Shankaracharya:

- Brahman is the sole reality, one without a second, eternal, conscious and infinite bliss. The world is an appearance, like a dream, on Brahman.

- The individual self (Jivatman) is really no different from Brahman, though it appears differentiated due to ignorance

(Avidya).

- By attaining the knowledge "I am Brahman" through scripture and a qualified teacher, the illusion is destroyed, and one realizes identity with the Supreme Self.

Atma Bodha (Knowledge of Self) by Shankaracharya:

- The body, senses, mind and intellect together constitute the "not-Self." They are insentient and ever-changing.

- The Atman, our true Self, is the witnessing consciousness, eternal, all-pervading and unattached.

- To realize one's true nature, spiritual practices like discrimination between Self and not-Self, desirelessness, and control of mind/senses are recommended.

Viveka Chudamani (Crest-Jewel of Discrimination) by Shankaracharya:

- The world experienced is a superimposition (Adhyasa) on Brahman, like a snake appearing on a rope due to ignorance.

- Attachment to the body, fear, and egoism arise from ignorance of our true Self which is existence-consciousness-bliss (Sat-Chit-Ananda).

- Freedom comes from clear discrimination (Viveka) between the eternal Self and the not-Self, abandoning desires, and abiding as the ever-present witnessing consciousness.

The essence from these texts is: We are not the body, mind or intellect but the infinite Atman/Brahman. By inquiring "Who am I ?" and gaining Self-knowledge from scripture and guru, the veil of ignorance dissolves. One then abides in the bliss of realizing one's true nature beyond all dualities and limitations.

These teachings guide the seeker to discriminate between the real and unreal, cultivate desirelessness and one-pointed focus to break free from bondage and suffering. The goal is the direct experience of one's divine Self and inseparable identity with the all-pervading Brahman - the lasting peace and freedom that is our very nature.

Several eminent spiritual masters and scholars have commented on the commonality of view presented in the texts Tattva Bodha,

Atma Bodha, and Viveka Chudamani, highlighting their unified message of Advaita Vedanta or non-dualism. Here are some notable commentaries:

1. Swami Vivekananda:

Vivekananda considered these three works by Adi Shankaracharya as quintessential texts expounding the philosophy of Advaita Vedanta. In his words, "Tattva Bodha, Atma Bodha and Viveka Chudamani are the perfect foundations to understand the lofty principles of non-dualism or Advaita."

2. Ramana Maharshi:

The renowned sage Ramana Maharshi often recommended the study of these texts to seekers. He saw them as complementary works that systematically unveil the reality of the Self (Atman) and its identity with Brahman. Ramana highlighted their emphasis on Self-inquiry (Atma-Vichara) as the direct path to Self-realization.

3. Swami Chinmayananda:

This influential teacher has written extensive commentaries on all three texts. He saw them as forming "a graded, integrated course of study" leading the seeker from basic discrimination to the experience of non-dual Brahman. Chinmayananda praised their scientific approach and lucid expression of profound Vedantic concepts.

4. Swami Dayananda Saraswati:

A renowned Advaita scholar, Dayananda viewed these works as masterpieces that comprehensively unfold the teaching of "Tat Tvam Asi" (That Thou Art). He appreciated how they employ different methods - reasoning, analogies, and contemplative techniques - to reveal the same ultimate truth of non-duality.

5. Nisargadatta Maharaj:

Though from the Nath tradition, Nisargadatta frequently quoted from these Advaitic texts in his teachings. He saw them as expounding the highest knowledge - that the world is an appearance on the substratum of the single, non-dual Self or Brahman.

While using slightly different language and emphasis, eminent exponents across traditions have recognized Tattva Bodha, Atma

Bodha and Viveka Chudamani as lucid, authoritative texts that provide a progressive, multi-faceted exposition of the core principles of Advaita Vedanta - the ultimate non-dualistic reality of Brahman/Atman and the means to realize it through knowledge and discrimination.

The teachings in Tattva Bodha, Atma Bodha and Viveka Chudamani share significant commonalities with the philosophy and practice outlined in Patanjali's Yoga Sutras.

Both systems ultimately point towards the realization of the true Self or Purusha, which is distinct from the mind-body complex.

In succeeding paragraphs, we attempt to map and integrate the key learnings from these Advaitic texts with the sadhana process suggested by Patanjali:

1. Discrimination between Purusha and Prakriti (Viveka):

Just as the Advaitic texts emphasize discriminating between the eternal Self (Atman) and the non-Self (body, mind, intellect), Patanjali's Yoga lays great importance on viveka - the ability to discern the conscious Purusha from unconscious Prakriti (nature/ manifested world).

2. Control of Chitta Vrittis (Mind Modifications):

The Advaitic teachings guide the seeker to go beyond the mind's conditioning and identifications. Patanjali's ashtanga yoga, especially the practices of ethical disciplines (yamas, niyamas), asanas, pranayama and pratyahara, serve to restrain and master the modifications of the mind (chitta vrittis).

3. Samadhi and Kaivalya (Liberation):

The ultimate goal in both Advaita Vedanta and Patanjali's Yoga is to abide in the true nature of the Self, free from all limitations. Samadhi, the state of unwavering concentration in Patanjali's system, aligns with the Advaitic vision of realizing one's identity with Brahman. Kaivalya or aloneness is akin to liberation from all dualities.

4. Need for Shravana, Manana and Nididhyasana:

The Advaitic texts emphasize studying scripture (shravana), reasoning (manana) and constant contemplation (nididhyasana) to uproot ignorance. Similarly, the Yoga Sutras prescribe the practices of study (svādhyāya) and contemplation on the Lord (Ishvara pranidhana) as key aids on the spiritual journey.

5. Role of the Guru and Satsang:

Both the Advaitic and Yoga traditions underline the importance of a realized Guru's guidance to remove doubts and provide the ultimate teachings. Association with truth-seekers (satsang) is also highlighted as contributing to progress on the path.

In essence, Patanjali's Raja Yoga can be seen as a comprehensive psycho-physical sadhana process to purify and prepare the mind-body vehicle for the ultimate realization of the Purusha or Atman, the changeless witnessing awareness expounded in the Advaitic texts.

The practices enable viveka (discrimination), vairagya (dispassion), removal of mental afflictions, and culminate in the direct experience of one's true nature, free from the notion of being the limited individual self.

The teachings in the Upanishads and other Hindu scriptures can be deeply understood and illuminated when viewed through the lens of the three seminal texts by Adi Shankaracharya - Tattva Bodha, Atma Bodha and Viveka Chudamani - as well as the Yoga Sutras of Patanjali. These later works systematize and elucidate the core principles found across the Upanishads and Vedic texts.

1. Non-duality of Brahman/Atman:

The Upanishadic mahavakyas like "Tat Tvam Asi" (That Thou Art) and "Aham Brahmasmi" (I am Brahman) point to the fundamental truth of non-dual Oneness between the individual self (Atman) and the cosmic Brahman. This is the central teaching expounded in Adi Shankara's Advaita treatises, providing a coherent philosophical framework.

2. Nature of the Self:

Descriptions in the Upanishads of the Atman as the eternal, consciousness principle distinct from the body-mind complex are systematically analyzed in Atma Bodha and Viveka Chudamani. These texts remove doubts about the true nature of the Self through reason and analogies.

3. World as Appearance:

The idea that the world is relatively unreal, a mere appearance (maya) on the substratum of Brahman is echoed in Tattva Bodha's analysis of the three states of experience - waking, dream and deep sleep. This aids in developing the discrimination between absolute and relative reality.

4. Means to Liberation:

The Upanishads recommend various spiritual practices like meditation, karma yoga, jnana yoga for Self-realization. Patanjali's Yoga Sutras synthesize these as the "yoga of action" (kriya yoga) and the "yoga of knowledge" (jnana yoga) as complementary means towards kaivalya (aloneness/liberation).

5. Guru and Shraddha:

Both the Upanishads and Advaitic texts like Viveka underscore the necessity of a realized Guru's guidance and shraddha (faith) in the teachings to remove doubts and ignorance obscuring Self-knowledge.

6. Ethical Disciplines:

The ethical injunctions (niyamas and yamas) outlined in Patanjali's ashtanga yoga system resonate with the virtues and codes of conduct emphasized across the Upanishads as prerequisites for spiritual evolution.

In essence, Adi Shankara's Prakarana Granthas and Patanjali's Yoga Darshana can be seen as coherent intellectual and practical maps that condense, synthesize and make accessible the profound wisdom of the ancient Upanishads and Vedic teachings on the path of Self-realization and spiritual illumination. They act as bridges to understand the spirit and essence of these venerable scriptures in a systematic manner.

Several modern eminent scholars and exponents of Vedanta have synthesized the learnings from the five primary sources - the Upanishads (Scriptures), Patanjali's Yoga Sutras, Tattva Bodha, Atma Bodha and Viveka Chudamani - in their teachings and writings. We see below how some key figures have integrated insights from these texts:

1. Swami Vivekananda:

Vivekananda saw the Yoga Sutras as providing a practical psychological framework complementing the philosophical Advaita teachings of the Upanishads and Shankara's treatises. He harmonized them, highlighting Patanjali's Raja Yoga as the "psychological process" and Vedanta the "metaphysical backdrop" for attaining liberation.

2. Sri Aurobindo:

Aurobindo viewed the Upanishads and Shankara's works as expressing the highest spiritual knowledge and experience. He drew parallels between the yogic discipline described by Patanjali and the triad of shravana-manana-nididhyasana emphasized in Viveka Chudamani for Self-realization.

3. Swami Sivananda:

A prolific integrator of various Hindu spiritual traditions, Sivananda synthesized the teachings of Vedanta, Yoga, and Tantra philosophies. He recommended studying the Upanishads, Gita, Shankara's Prakarana works and Patanjali's Sutras together as a "gateway to the Absolute."

4. Swami Chinmayananda:

One of the foremost modern expositors of Advaita Vedanta, Chinmayananda's teachings and commentaries seamlessly wove in principles and practices from the Upanishads, Bhagavad Gita, Shankara's treatises and Patanjali's Yoga system. He presented them as complementary aids for "conscious spiritual living."

5. Swami Dayananda Saraswati:

An authority on Advaita philosophy, Dayananda harmonized the core teachings across texts like the Upanishads, Brahma Sutras, Viveka Chudamani and Yoga Sutras. He viewed the four primary spiritual practices (sadhana chatushtaya) mentioned across these works as an integrated approach for Self-knowledge.

6. Swami Satchidanandendra Saraswati:

This renowned Advaita scholar and teacher provided an insightful synthesis, highlighting how Shankara's works elucidate the Upanishadic teachings, while Patanjali's Yoga complemented Advaita by describing methods to prepare the mind for assimilating Self-knowledge.

The common thread is viewing the Upanishads as the loftiest scriptural source expounding non-dual Brahman, while the texts by Shankara and Patanjali provide an intellectual framework and practical disciplines to realize those ultimate truths in one's experience. By integrating these sources, modern scholars have presented Vedanta as a comprehensive knowledge system for spiritual illumination.

In next and concluding chapter 14, we continues this synthesis process in an intutive manner and attemp;t to suggest a way forward for the seeker.

FOURTEEN

WAY FORWARD FOR A SEEKER

Hari Om

Using the insight provided in the previous chapter 13 and key learnings from previous 11 chapters, we have prepared **Figure 1** below.

Basic Concepts from Hindu Scriptures (Chapters 2,3,4)

- Karma Theory and Rebirth
- Role of free will and possibility of Moksha
- Guru's role as embodiment of knowledge
- Five Koshas of personality and need to go beyond all five using discrimination to realize True Self

Patanjali Yoga Sutra (Chapters 5,6,7,8,9)

- Eight Limbs of Yoga
- Importance of Ethical and Disciplined living in Sadhna process
- Faith in a Higher reality
- Need for consistent practice without distraction to manifested special power

Patanjali Yoga Sutra

1. Eight Limbs of Yoga

2. Importance of Ethical and Disciplined living in Sadhna process

3. Faith in a Higher reality

4. Need for consistent practice without distraction to manifested special powers

Scriptures

1, Karma Theory and Rebirth

2. Role of free will and possibility of Moksha

3. Guru's role as embodiment of knowledge

3. Five Koshas of personality and need to go beyond all five using discrimination to realise True Self

Vivek Chudamani

1. Cultivate discrimination (Viveka)

2. Practice detachment (Vairagya)

3. Develop virtues (Shatsampat)

4. Study the scriptures (Sravana)

5. Practice meditation (Nididhyasana)

6. Serve selflessly (Karma Yoga)

7. Cultivate devotion (Bhakti)

Synthesis of Key Learnings

1. Ultimate goal of life is realising identity with Brahman

2. Ethical behaviour and discipline are key to reach it

3. Faith in higher power and use of Discrimination and Dispassion are essential

4. Maintaining Equanimity

5. Grace of Guru and the higher power manifested through him is crucial

6. Continuity of practice even over several life cycles is a norm

7. Practice of Four Fold path (Four sadhana chatushtaya)

8. Development of 6 Virtues (Shatsampat)

Tattva Bodha

1. Brahman as ultimate reality

2. Nature of Self and its identity with Brahman

3. Knowledge, Discrimination and Dispassion

4. Four fold path

5. The Stages of Self-Realization

6. The State of Liberation (Moksha)

Atma Bodha

1. Cultivating Self-Awareness

2. Practicing Discrimination (Viveka)

3. Developing Dispassion (Vairagya)

4. Pursuing Self-Knowledge (Atma-jnana)

5. Seeking Guidance (Guru-Upadesha)

6. Maintaining Equanimity

7. Living with Integrity

Figure 1: Synthesis of Learning from Previous Eleven Chapters

Tattva Bodha (Chapter 10)

- Brahman as ultimate reality
- Nature of Self and its identity with Brahman
- Knowledge, Discrimination and Dispassion
- Four fold path (sadhana chatushtaya)- The pillars are Viveka (knowing the difference between self and no-self), vairagya (non-attachment), shatsampat* (attain a balance between mental and emotional in order to see things as they truly are), and mumukshutva (desire to achieve freedom from suffering).

*The details of shatsampat (six virtues) are:

Sama (Mastery over the mind) ,

Dama (Control of the external senses),

Uparati (Observance of one's own dharma (duties)),

Titiksha (Endurance of opposites (heat and cold, pleasure and pain, etc)) ,

Sraddha (Reverential Faith in the words of the Scriptures and the Guru)

Samadhana (Focussing or single-pointedness of the mind).

Vivek Chudamani (Chapter 11)

- Cultivate discrimination (Viveka)
- Practice detachment (Vairagya)
- Develop virtues (Shatsampat)
- Study the scriptures (Sravana)
- Practice meditation (Nididhyasana)
- Serve selflessly (Karma Yoga)
- Cultivate devotion (Bhakti)

Atma Bodha (Chapter 12)

- Cultivating Self-Awareness
- Practicing Discrimation (Vivea)
- Developing Dispassion (Vairagya)
- Pursuing Self-Knowledge (Atma-jnana)
- Seeking Guidance (Guru-Upadesha)
- Maintaining Equanimity
- Living with Integrity

Synthesis of Key Learnings

- Ultimate goal of life is realising identity with Brahman
- Ethical behaviour and discipline are key to reach it
- Faith in higher power and use of Discrimination and Dispassion are essential
- Maintaining Equanimity
- Grace of Guru and the higher power manifested through him is crucial
- Continuity of practice even over several life cycles is a norm

- Practice of Four Fold path (Four sadhana chatushtaya)
- Development of 6 Virtues (Shatsampat)

For a seeker treading the path of spirituality and Self-realization, the learnings from the five primary sources - the Upanishads, Patanjali's Yoga Sutras, Tattva Bodha, Atma Bodha and Viveka Chudamani - can possibly be embraced and integrated into daily life in the following ways:

1. Study and Reflection (Svadhyaya):

Regular study and contemplation of these sacred texts is the foundation. Setting aside daily time for svadhyaya - whether reading/listening to the original verses or commentaries - allows the teachings to penetrate the intellect.

2. Discrimination (Viveka):

Cultivating the ability to discriminate between the eternal Self and the impermanent non-Self, as emphasized in texts like Viveka Chudamani. Applying this viveka in every experience and constantly asking "Who am I?" in the midst of daily activities.

3. Ethical Disciplines (Yamas and Niyamas):

Imbibing and practicing the ethical restraints (yamas) and observances (niyamas) prescribed by Patanjali as prerequisites for spiritual growth. This lays the foundation for an effective sadhana.

4. Meditation and Contemplation:

Developing a daily practice of meditation as delineated in the Yoga Sutras and other texts. This can involve techniques like mantras, breath awareness, or the profound contemplation (nididhyasana) on profound Upanishadic statements like "I am Brahman."

5. Karma Yoga:

Performing all duties and actions in a spirit of selflessness and offering them to the Divine, as taught in texts like the Bhagavad Gita. This cultivates detachment and purifies the mind.

6. Seeking Guidance:

Regularly seeking the association (satsang) of realized guru figures who can remove doubts, provide instructions, and share realizations from their direct experience of the ultimate teachings.

7. Introspection and Self-Inquiry:

Setting aside time for regular self-inquiry and introspection in the manner of "Who am I?" as advocated by Adi Shankara to turn the mind inward from identification with objects.

8. Developing Qualities:

Consciously striving to inculcate the qualities conducive to Self-realization like humility, dispassion, perseverance, tranquility, self-control as outlined by various texts.

The key is to make spiritual sadhana an integrated and vibrant part of one's daily routine and not merely an event. With sincerity, commitment and the blessings of the guru's grace, steady and sustained practice of the teachings can ultimately culminate in the direct realization of the Self.

Swami Krishnananda of Divine Society in his book titled **'Spiritual Aspiration and Practice'** has provided for a seeker very deep insights on the 3 components , Viveka, Vairagya and Shatsampat of four fold path(sadhana chatushtaya) and we reproduce it below for benefit of the reader.

*"**Viveka and vairagya** are more of an intellectual and rationalistic nature, where you have to exercise your understanding and logical thinking much more than anything else.*

But there is something else, which is called your feelings. "Whatever be the thing you say, I want this." This is what the heart of hearts will tell you. This heart has also to be disciplined in the same way as the intellect has to be disciplined through viveka and vairagya. Your heart is yourself. Your brain and intellect are not so connected with your existence as your feelings and heart. "My heart is what I am." Now, this third requisite is called shad-sampat, the acquisition of six virtues. They are called sampat because they are actually treasures, very valuable things. The six virtues are sama, dama, uparati, titiksha, sraddha and samadhana.

***Sama** is a determination on your part to be always calm and quiet under any kind of condition, even aggressive conditions. It is very important. Hate does not cease by hate. Hate ceases by love. Reaction is* *not the way in which you have to conduct yourself towards an action. Two persons are necessary to quarrel, and you need not be a party in that. Restrain your mind with the help of the understanding that you have already exercised through viveka and vairagya.*

***Sama is** the restraint of the internal organ, which is the mind, and dama is the restraint of the sense organs, the discipline of the organs outside. There is a distinction between the internal organ and the external organs. The internal organ, or the psyche proper, is called the antahkarana chatushtaya. Mano buddhi ahankara chitta: the mind that thinks, the buddhi or intellect that decides and determines, the ahankara that identifies everything with itself, and the chitta or memory that remembers past things; these are, broadly speaking, the functional aspects of the psyche. Because they are four, they are called chatushtaya; and because it is an internal faculty, it is called antahkarana, not external. That is the mind. In Western psychology, the word 'mind' is used for all these four aspects. Sometimes they divide the mind into understanding, feeling and willing. This is the limitation of psychology in Western thought. But there is much more about the mind than only this threefold classification. So much about the internal organ, about which we said sama is to be exercised.*

***Dama is** the restraint of the five organs—the eyes, the ears and sensations of every kind. There are five senses of knowledge and five organs of action. The eyes have a passion to see certain things, and there is a passion for every sense organ. Passion is an uncontrollable desire. A desire that has overcome you and flooded you is called passion. Desire is the beginning stage of an overwhelming, consuming longing. Desires insinuate themselves into you gradually, like diseases that crop up inside without your knowing that they are there and manifest themselves only afterwards through the body."*

Embracing the comprehensive wisdom from the Upanishads, Shankara's Advaitic texts and Patanjali's Yoga system provides the seeker the philosophical depth, ethical and mental anchors, and yogic practices for the ultimate attainment of moksha - the state of freedom, peace and oneness

The spiritual journey is a very personal experience and progress would depend greatly on our circumstances in life. All of us are propelled by the past life Samskaras and the role of 'free will' is considered very crucial in changing the trajectory of our destiny towards liberation.

It may not be out of place to share some salient and relevant points from my personal experience on this journey.

I was born in a religious family and my parents believed in God and regular Puja (ceremonial worship) was part of my routine too. As I grew up, my interest to know more on this subject increased and during college days , I tried to make sense by reading some rudimentary books on religion and philosophy. However, after joining the Indian Air Force , my daily routine for spiritual quest suffered a setback as I was attempting to adapt to a new way of life and as a bachelor, officer mess living had its own compulsions.

Marriage brought a change and as my wife also had interest in religiuos practices, a notable change came in my routine but any serious attempt at Spirituality was a distant dream.

However, it was only after our second daughter was born that, by providence, during my Delhi posting, I had a chance to listen to Shri Vethathiri Maharishi in a small gathering at someone's place where I had taken my father to attend the talk.

My father was retired by then from Indian Railways service and was into Spirituality, having been meditating for many years. I felt motivated to listen to more of my future Guruji's talks and finally he was kind enough to initiate me into Simplified Kundalini Yoga.

During this period, I was pursuing MTech. course at IIT Delhi. This permitted me to join group meditation on a weekly basis being organised by other aspirants of meditation.

It certainly helped me. Starting from that first step and my effort to read books related to Spirituality, life moved on.

I would be honest to mention that the various approaches to progress on this path as indicated in the relevant texts were, however, not fully integrated in my life. Availability of books on Patanjali Yoga Sutra, besides other scriptures from Gita press

Gorakhpur at home, helped me get some further nsights.

Because of my father's deep interest in practice of spirituality and his proclivity to buy books and discuss the issues covered during our informal discussions at home was a conducive factor.

My mother was also very religious and used to do her Puja and Dhyan with very deep devotion. These enabling factors did help me and the meditation continued although with lack of focus.

Only after retirement, I could bring regularity to meditation. My wife and I participated in a few Spiritual activities under the aegis of well known names in this domain.

Only in the last couple of years, my interest has picked up intensity and I am able to practice meditation twice a day on a sustainable basis. All I can say with due humility is that it is the grace of God combined with our continuous baby steps in this journey that are very crucial.

I feel the methodology described in various texts covered in this book are indeed effective and one needs to imbibe them as feasible with all sincerity and deep faith in the God almighty.

The intense desire to achieve the ultimate goal of self realization should override all other social priorities. One certainly should fulfill one's family and social responsibilities without any compromise and attempt to lead an ethical life.

Purpose of sharing the above facts of my journey is to motivate the new entrants to not lose heart and continue on this glorious path which can be considered as epitome of our life as human beings.

In the end, I pray to almighty God to bless you all with His grace. Hari Om

Online Resources

Chapter 1- Setting the Context

https://www.swami-krishnananda.org/

Chapter 2 - Basic Concepts from Hindu Scripture

Vedanta

https://youtu.be/AawWsJNi0gM?si=_l1rZNbw58hG4DiK

Meditation

https://youtu.be/wm9gomNUi48?si=vpBiCCcOddERE_an

Karma Yoga

https://youtu.be/-rgNWIeF9Qo?si=bZuL3MHorWjfljhd

Jnana Yoga

https://youtu.be/EijmfagFw20?si=3RbXyaNXKg0AkrB6

Chapter 3- Concept of Rebirth

Cycle of reincarnation

https://youtu.be/kkMbbrOR1qw?si=tGcRkK_6vy0DFwF_

Chapter 4 - Who am I really? Panch Kosha Viveka

The Secret of the Five Sheaths by Swami Sarvapriyananda

https://youtu.be/rPtHCCT1SZM?si=iuM0AnUWHgf6VS0H

Chapter 5- Journey towards our true self -The Patanjali Yoga Sutra

Who is Patanjali? What is Yoga?

https://youtu.be/Bc5UHKO3wWc?si=G4NkgSeZqPlAFdrW

Patanjali Yoga Sutras by Swami Nikhilanand Sarswati- Day 1 | Samadhi Pada - Introduction Talk

https://youtu.be/vE94dzkgh2A?si=Rs0YJGY2hmttFGRm

Chapter 6 - How to begin the inward journey? Sadhana Essentials

Patanjali Yoga Sutra - Wikipedia

https://www.scribd.com/document/514278851/

Yoga-Sutras-of-Patanjali-Wikipedia

https://en.wikipedia.org/wiki/Yoga_Sutras_of_Patanjali

Basic concepts of Kriya Yoga

https://youtu.be/ohr8reh_AqE?si=oLvHXY7bbaqqE3r4

Foundations of Kriya Yoga

https://youtu.be/GTIKrXpwBTI?si=r-N3naxjZ9yKVU1L

Chapter 7 -Samadhi Process - How the true self is reached?

Play list of 11 videos by Swami Nikhilananda Saraswati on Samadhi Pada

https://youtube.com/

playlist?list=

PLZx3LBhP9JWSFjlPqDxHNLdAXZQy-0JPT&si=Wmmz7y-sRIq1F75e

Chapter 8 - Spiritual Powers of a Yogi - Vibhuti Pada

1. Vibhuti Pada Introduction video from Vivekananda Rock Memorial

https://youtu.be/3TpZ_7bTsiU?si=4DpPuCeyToppFn1a

2. Full playlist of 172 videos on Patanjali Yoga Sutras from Vivekananda Rock Memorial. 55 videos pertaining to Vibhuti Pada appear

after Samadhi and Sadhna Pada videos. Highly recommended.

https://youtube.com/

playlist?list=

PLM4rzq7OuKeJN3kxPKgMlY8U_KBktmSYj&si=5kcc5K5qae0MC3lz

Chapter 9 - A Liberated Yogi – Kaivalya Pada

Kaivalya Pada Introduction video from Vivekananda Rock Memorial

https://youtu.be/jAMyiZKkXB8?si=uReM87_LB6NYKRSm

Patanjali Yoga Sutra videos playlist of 172 videos from Vivekananda Rock Memorial. Kaivalya Pada is described in 34 final videos after initial videos pertaining to Samadhi, Sadhna and Vibhuti Padas.

https://youtube.com/

playlist?list=

PLM4rzq7OuKeJN3kxPKgMlY8U_KBktmSYj&si=BZjXGBDeQLcOXZtg

Chapter 10 - The Awakening to Reality - Tattva Bodha

Tattva Bodha by Anubhavanand playlist of 7 videos.

https://youtbe.com/

playlist?list=

PLAF_c2xr3i8DKWyTTr0z_eRgB4IW-vvcS&si=1oOdRqEEnw88rtQR

Chapter 11 - Our Spiritual Compass-- Vivek Chudamani

Swami Anubhavananda playlist of 9 videos on Vivekachoodamani

https://youtube.com/

playlist?list=

PLAF_c2xr3i8CXOOELLFYLCa4NQOMUfdZg&si=67ygD3fqSsLRP8bi

Swami Tyagananda playlist of 60 videos on Vivekachoodamani

https://youtube.com/

playlist?list=

PLWjpkY4mU2RDyl7Wxx2v7LN8BDoC_Ir0d&si=u0blBp9hE-lVYMZr

Chapter 12 - Who am I ? -Atma Bodha (Knowledge of Self)

Swami Anubhavananda playlist of 17 videos on Atma bodha

https://youtube.com/

playlist?list=

PLAF_c2xr3i8ASTRVs-8RTMMHQjg4OGnVv&si=lyyAUp5X9EhByx2S

Chapter 13 - Synthesis of the Learning so far

https://www.swami-krishnananda.org/

Chapter 14 - Way Forward

https://www.swami-krishnananda.org/

Bibliography

Patanjali's Yoga Sutras:

1. Bryant, E. F. (2009). The Yoga Sutras of Patanjali: A New Edition, Translation, and Commentary. North Point Press.

2. Iyengar, B. K. S. (2002). Light on the Yoga Sutras of Patanjali. Thorsons.

3. Satchidananda, S. (2012). The Yoga Sutras of Patanjali: Commentary on the Raja Yoga Sutras. Integral Yoga Publications.

4. Feuerstein, G. (1989). The Yoga-Sutra of Patanjali: A New Translation and Commentary. Inner Traditions.

5. Desikachar, T. K. V. (2003). Reflections on Yoga Sutras of Patanjali. Krishnamacharya Yoga Mandiram.

Tattva Bodha:

6. Chinmayananda, S. (2008). Tattva Bodha of Adi Sankara. Chinmaya Publications.

7. Dayananda, S. (2004). Tattva Bodha: An Introduction to Vedanta. Vision Books.

8. Nikhilananda, S. (1967). Ātmabodha and Tattva-bodha of Śankarāchārya. Sri Ramakrishna Math.

Vivek Chudamani:

9. Chinmayananda, S. (2005). Vivekachudamani of Shankaracharya. Central Chinmaya Mission Trust.

10. Prabhavananda, S., & Isherwood, C. (1978). Shankara's Crest-Jewel of Discrimination. Vedanta Press.

11. Grimes, J. (2004). The Vivekacūḍāmaṇi of Śaṅkarācārya Bhagavatpāda: An Introduction and Translation. Ashgate.

Atma Bodha:

12. Nikhilananda, S. (1946). Self-Knowledge: An English Translation of Sankaracharya's Atmabodha. Ramakrishna-Vivekananda Center.

13. Chinmayananda, S. (2006). Atma Bodha of Adi Sankara. Central Chinmaya Mission Trust.

14. Sastry, A. M. (1897). Âtma-Bodha of Sri Sankarâchârya. Theosophical Publishing House.

Brahma Sutras:

15. Thibaut, G. (1890). The Vedânta Sûtras with the Commentary of Sankarâkârya. Oxford University Press.

16. Vireswarananda, S. (1936). Brahma Sutras: According to Sri Sankara. Advaita Ashrama.

17. Sivananda, S. (1977). Brahma Sutras. Divine Life Society.

18. Radhakrishnan, S. (1960). The Brahma Sutra: The Philosophy of Spiritual Life. George Allen & Unwin.

Bhagavad Gita:

19. Easwaran, E. (2007). The Bhagavad Gita (Classics of Indian Spirituality). Nilgiri Press.

20. Zaehner, R. C. (1969). The Bhagavad-Gītā. Oxford University Press.

21. Radhakrishnan, S. (1948). The Bhagavadgita. Harper & Brothers.

22. Deutsch, E., & van Buitenen, J. A. B. (1968). A Source Book of Advaita Vedanta. University of Hawaii Press.

23. Sargeant, W. (2009). The Bhagavad Gita: Twenty-fifth-Anniversary Edition. SUNY Press.

11 Main Upanishads:

24. Olivelle, P. (1998). The Early Upanishads: Annotated Text and Translation. Oxford University Press.

25. Radhakrishnan, S. (1953). The Principal Upanishads. Harper.

26. Nikhilananda, S. (1949). The Upanishads: A New Translation (4 volumes). Harper.

27. Hume, R. E. (1921). The Thirteen Principal Upanishads. Oxford University Press.

28. Müller, F. M. (1879-1884). The Upanishads (Sacred Books of the East, vols. 1 & 15). Oxford University Press.

General Studies and Commentaries:

29. Dasgupta, S. (1922-1955). A History of Indian Philosophy (5 volumes). Cambridge University Press.

30. Potter, K. H. (Ed.). (1981-2015). Encyclopedia of Indian Philosophies (multiple volumes). Princeton University Press.

31. Hiriyanna, M. (1932). Outlines of Indian Philosophy. George Allen & Unwin.

32. Deussen, P. (1906). The Philosophy of the Upanishads. T. & T. Clark.

33. Sharma, C. (2000). A Critical Survey of Indian Philosophy. Motilal Banarsidass.

34. Flood, G. (1996). An Introduction to Hinduism. Cambridge University Press.

Appendix A : Hindu Scriptures And Upanishads

Basic concepts from Hindu scriptures

Here are some of the key concepts from Hindu scriptures that are relevant for self-realization:

1. Brahman - The ultimate, formless, infinite reality that is the source of all existence. Realizing one's true identity as Brahman is the goal of self-realization.

2. Atman - The individual soul or innermost essence. According to Advaita Vedanta, realizing that the Atman is identical with Brahman is self-realization.

3. Maya - The illusory power that causes the world of multiplicity and ignorance to appear as reality, obscuring the true non-dual nature of Brahman.

4. Avidya - Spiritual ignorance or lack of true knowledge about one's real nature as Brahman. Overcoming avidya through vidya (knowledge) is essential.

5. Karma - The law of cause and effect governing one's actions and their consequences, binding the soul to the cycle of birth and rebirth (samsara).

6. Moksha - The final liberation from the cycle of rebirth, the state of freedom and unity with the Absolute Brahman.

7. Jnana Yoga - The path of knowledge and wisdom to discriminate between the real and unreal, leading to self-realization.

8. Karma Yoga - The path of selfless action, performing duties without attachment to the fruits, as a means of self-purification.

9. Bhakti Yoga - The path of devotion, love and surrender to the Divine as a means to transcend the ego and realize one's true nature.

10. Yoga - The various spiritual practices like meditation, contemplation, ethical disciplines to still the mind and attain self-realization.

11. Purushartha - The four goals of human life - Dharma (righteous living), Artha (prosperity), Kama (pleasure) and Moksha

(liberation).

12. Viveka - The power of discrimination to distinguish between the real and unreal, permanent and impermanent, leading to self-knowledge.

13. Jivanmukta - The state of being liberated while still in the body, having realized one's true self.

14. Guru - The spiritual teacher or guide who imparts the knowledge and assists in the journey of self-realization.

The essence is to shed ignorance through the various paths - knowledge, devotion, ethical living and yogic practices - to realize one's true nature as the eternal, blissful Brahman or Atman. This self-realization is portrayed as the ultimate goal in Hindu scriptures.

1. Brihadaranyaka Upanishad

This is one of the oldest and most important Upanishads. It's associated with the Yajurveda and discusses the nature of reality, consciousness, and the self (Atman).

Scholar's comment:

Dr. Anantanand Rambachan, Professor of Religion at St. Olaf College, notes: "The Brihadaranyaka Upanishad is foundational in its exposition of non-duality (advaita) and its famous 'neti neti' (not this, not this) teaching about the nature of Brahman."

2. Chandogya Upanishad

Associated with the Samaveda, this Upanishad is known for its teachings on the nature of Brahman and the famous statement "Tat Tvam Asi" (You are That).

Scholar's comment:

Swami Sarvapriyananda of the Ramakrishna Order states: "The Chandogya Upanishad's exposition of 'Tat Tvam Asi' is perhaps the most direct pointer to the non-dual nature of reality and the individual's true identity with Brahman."

3. Isha Upanishad

This short but profound Upanishad is associated with the Yajurveda and emphasizes the unity of all existence.

Scholar's comment:

Dr. David Frawley (Vamadeva Shastri) observes: "The Isha Upanishad beautifully reconciles spiritual knowledge with worldly life, showing how to live in the world while recognizing its divine nature."

4. Kena Upanishad

Associated with the Samaveda, this Upanishad explores the nature of Brahman and the limits of intellectual knowledge in understanding ultimate reality.

Scholar's comment:

Dr. Jeffery Long, Professor of Religion and Asian Studies at Elizabethtown College, notes: "The Kena Upanishad powerfully illustrates the limitations of human intellect in grasping the ultimate reality, emphasizing the need for direct spiritual experience."

5. Katha Upanishad

This Upanishad, associated with the Yajurveda, contains the famous dialogue between Nachiketa and Yama (the god of death) about the nature of the self and death.

Scholar's comment:

Sadhguru Jaggi Vasudev remarks: "The Katha Upanishad's dialogue between Nachiketa and Yama is a profound exploration of life, death, and the nature of consciousness that remains deeply relevant today."

6. Mundaka Upanishad

Associated with the Atharvaveda, this Upanishad distinguishes between lower and higher knowledge and emphasizes the importance of direct realization.

Scholar's comment:

Dr. Anantanand Rambachan states: "The Mundaka Upanishad's distinction between para and apara vidya (higher and lower knowledge) is crucial for understanding the Vedantic approach to knowledge and liberation."

7. Mandukya Upanishad

This concise Upanishad, associated with the Atharvaveda, is known for its analysis of the states of consciousness and the sacred syllable Om.

Scholar's comment:

Swami Sarvapriyananda notes: "The Mandukya Upanishad's exposition of the four states of consciousness provides a profound framework for understanding the nature of reality and the self."

8. Prashna Upanishad

Associated with the Atharvaveda, this Upanishad is structured as a series of questions and answers about the nature of reality and the self.

Scholar's comment:

Dr. Jeffery Long observes: "The question-answer format of the Prashna Upanishad reflects the dialogical nature of Indian philosophy and the importance of inquiry in spiritual growth."

9. Taittiriya Upanishad

This Upanishad, associated with the Yajurveda, is known for its teachings on the five sheaths (koshas) of the self and the bliss of Brahman.

Scholar's comment:

Dr. David Frawley states: "The Taittiriya Upanishad's teaching on the five koshas provides a comprehensive model for understanding the different layers of human existence and consciousness."

10. Aitareya Upanishad

Associated with the Rigveda, this Upanishad discusses the nature of Atman and the process of creation.

Scholar's comment:

Swami Vivekananda (in his commentary): "The Aitareya Upanishad presents a unique perspective on creation, emphasizing the primacy of consciousness in the cosmic process."

11. Shvetashvatara Upanishad

This Upanishad, associated with the Yajurveda, is notable for its theistic orientation and its discussion of yoga and meditation.

Scholar's comment:

Dr. Edwin Bryant, Professor of Hinduism at Rutgers University, notes: "The Shvetashvatara Upanishad is significant for its integration of Samkhya, Yoga, and Vedanta philosophies, and its theistic orientation that influenced later bhakti traditions."

These Upanishads form the core of Vedantic philosophy and continue to be studied and interpreted by scholars and spiritual seekers worldwide. Their teachings on the nature of reality, consciousness, and the self remain profoundly influential in contemporary spirituality and philosophy.

Impact of the main Upanishads on Spirituality discourse and utility in daily life is discussed below.

1. Brihadaranyaka Upanishad Influence:

This Upanishad has profoundly shaped the non-dualistic (Advaita) school of Vedanta. Its teachings on the nature of reality and consciousness have been central to Indian philosophical discourse for centuries.

Daily life application: The concept of "neti neti" (not this, not this) can be applied to cultivate detachment from material possessions and transient experiences. It encourages us to look beyond surface-level appearances and seek deeper meaning in life.

2. Chandogya Upanishad Influence:

The mahavakya (great saying) "Tat Tvam Asi" (You are That) has become a cornerstone of Advaita Vedanta philosophy, influencing countless spiritual seekers in their quest for self-realization.

Daily life application: Recognizing our fundamental unity with all existence can foster compassion and reduce ego-driven behaviors. It can help us treat others with more kindness and respect.

3. Isha Upanishad

Influence: This Upanishad has significantly impacted the understanding of how to balance spiritual pursuit with worldly responsibilities.

Daily life application: Its teaching of "Ishavasyam idam sarvam" (All this is inhabited by the Divine) can help us approach our daily tasks and interactions with reverence and mindfulness, seeing the sacred in the ordinary.

4. Kena Upanishad

Influence: This Upanishad has shaped discussions on the limits of intellectual knowledge in spiritual matters, emphasizing the importance of direct experience.

Daily life application: It reminds us to remain humble in our pursuit of knowledge and to value experiential understanding over mere intellectual grasp. This can lead to a more open-minded and experiential approach to life.

5. Katha Upanishad

Influence: Its exploration of death and the nature of the self has deeply influenced Hindu and Buddhist thought on these subjects.

Daily life application: The story of Nachiketa teaches us about the value of persistence in spiritual seeking. It also encourages us to contemplate the transient nature of life, potentially leading to more meaningful prioritization of our time and energy.

6. Mundaka Upanishad

Influence: Its distinction between lower and higher knowledge has shaped educational philosophy in spiritual contexts.

Daily life application: This teaching can guide us in balancing practical, worldly knowledge with the pursuit of higher spiritual understanding. It encourages lifelong learning and spiritual growth.

7. Mandukya Upanishad

Influence: Its analysis of the states of consciousness and the meaning of Om has been crucial in both philosophical discourse and meditation practices.

Daily life application: Understanding different states of consciousness can help us be more aware of our mental states throughout the day. The meditation on Om can be a practical tool for stress reduction and inner peace.

8. Prashna Upanishad

Influence: Its question-answer format has influenced pedagogical methods in spiritual teaching.

Daily life application: It encourages us to cultivate a questioning mind and not to accept spiritual teachings blindly. This approach can lead to a more genuine and personally meaningful spiritual practice.

9. Taittiriya Upanishad

Influence: Its teaching on the five sheaths of existence has influenced both philosophical understanding and yogic practices.

Daily life application: Awareness of these sheaths can guide holistic self-care, encouraging attention to physical, energetic, mental, intellectual, and spiritual aspects of our being.

10. Aitareya Upanishad

Influence: Its perspective on creation and consciousness has informed various schools of Indian philosophy.

Daily life application: Its emphasis on consciousness can encourage us to be more aware of our thoughts and actions, potentially leading to more mindful and intentional living.

11. Shvetashvatara Upanishad

Influence: Its integration of various philosophical strands and its theistic orientation have influenced both monistic and dualistic schools of thought, as well as later bhakti (devotional) movements.

Daily life application: Its teachings on yoga and meditation provide practical tools for stress management and spiritual growth. Its theistic elements can provide a framework for those inclined towards devotional practices in daily life.

Overall, these Upanishads have collectively shaped the landscape of Indian spirituality and continue to offer profound insights applicable to modern life. They encourage self-reflection, ethical living, and the pursuit of higher consciousness - all of which can contribute to a more meaningful and balanced life in our complex, fast-paced world.

The key is to approach these ancient teachings not as abstract philosophy, but as practical guides for living. By contemplating and gradually incorporating their wisdom into our daily routines, decisions, and interactions, we can potentially experience greater peace, purpose, and connection in our lives.

Appendix B : Brief Introduction To Brahma Sutras

Brahma Sutra

The Brahma Sutras, also known as the Vedanta Sutras, are a foundational text of Hindu philosophy composed by the sage Veda Vyasa. Here are some of the key concepts outlined in the Brahma Sutras:

1. Brahman: The central concept is Brahman, the ultimate, formless, infinite reality that is the source of all existence. The Sutras aim to establish the nature of Brahman and Its relationship with the world and individual souls.

2. Cause and Effect: The Sutras analyze the cause-and-effect relationship between Brahman and the universe, exploring various theories like Brahman being the material and efficient cause (Parinama-vada) or the world being an apparent manifestation of Brahman (Vivarta-vada).

3. Jagat (The World): The Sutras discuss the nature of the world, whether it is real or an illusion (Maya), and its dependence on Brahman for its existence and sustenance.

4. Jiva (Individual Soul): The text explores the nature of the individual soul (Jiva), its relationship with Brahman, and the process of attaining liberation (Moksha) from the cycle of birth and death.

5. Karma and Rebirth: The law of Karma and the cycle of rebirth (Samsara) are discussed, along with the means to break free from this cycle through knowledge of Brahman.

6. Means of Knowledge: The Sutras analyze different means of attaining knowledge of Brahman, such as perception, inference, scripture (Shruti), and direct realization (Anubhava).

7. Adhikaranas (Topics): The Brahma Sutras are structured as adhikaranas or topics, each consisting of a statement (Vishaya), a doubt (Samshaya), and a conclusion (Siddhanta).

8. Reconciliation of Contradictions: The text attempts to reconcile apparent contradictions within the Upanishads and Vedic

scriptures through various interpretations and explanations.

9. Schools of Vedanta: The Sutras provide a foundation for the development of different schools of Vedanta philosophy, such as Advaita (non-dualism), Vishishtadvaita (qualified non-dualism), and Dvaita (dualism).

The Brahma Sutras are considered a crucial text in the Prasthanatrayi (trio of foundational texts) of Hindu philosophy, along with the Upanishads and the Bhagavad Gita. They systematically present the philosophical concepts of Vedanta and have been extensively commented upon by various Acharyas (teachers) over the centuries.

Implications for Daily Life:

1. Self-reflection and inquiry:

The Brahma Sutra encourages deep self-inquiry. In daily life, this translates to regularly questioning our assumptions, beliefs, and the nature of our experiences.

Application: Set aside time each day for introspection and self-analysis.

2. Unity in diversity:

Understanding the non-dual nature of reality can foster a sense of unity and interconnectedness with all beings.

Application: Practice seeing the divine in everyone and everything, promoting compassion and empathy in daily interactions.

3. Ethical living:

The text emphasizes the importance of righteous living as a prerequisite for spiritual growth.

Application: Make conscious choices in alignment with ethical principles in personal and professional life.

4. Mindfulness:

The Brahma Sutra's teachings on the nature of reality encourage being fully present and aware.

Application: Practice mindfulness in daily activities, from eating to working.

5. Detachment:

Understanding the temporary nature of worldly experiences can help cultivate healthy detachment.

Application: Practice non-attachment to outcomes while still putting in your best effort

6. Continuous learning:

The text's systematic approach to knowledge encourages lifelong learning and questioning.

Application: Cultivate a habit of regular study and intellectual engagement with philosophical ideas.

7. Meditation:

The Brahma Sutra emphasizes meditation as a means to realize the ultimate truth.

Application: Incorporate a regular meditation practice into your daily routine.

8. Harmony of thought and action:

The text stresses the importance of aligning one's understanding with one's actions.

Application: Strive to bring your daily actions in line with your highest understanding and beliefs.

9. Overcoming ego:

Understanding the true nature of self can help in transcending ego-driven behaviors.

Application: Practice humility and selflessness in daily interactions.

10. Seeking guidance:

The Brahma Sutra tradition emphasizes the importance of a qualified teacher.

Application: Seek wisdom from mentors and teachers in various aspects of life.

11. Cultivating discernment:

The text's logical approach encourages developing a discerning mind.

Application: Practice critical thinking and discernment in daily decision-making.

12. Balancing worldly and spiritual pursuits:

While focusing on the ultimate reality, the text doesn't negate worldly responsibilities.

Application: Strive to balance material pursuits with spiritual growth in daily life.

Contemporary Relevance:

Despite its ancient origins, the Brahma Sutra remains relevant in addressing fundamental questions about existence, consciousness, and the nature of reality. Its teachings can provide a framework for dealing with modern challenges such as stress, existential anxiety, and the search for meaning in a fast-paced world.

Many contemporary spiritual teachers and philosophers continue to draw inspiration from the Brahma Sutra, interpreting its ancient wisdom in the context of modern life. Its emphasis on inquiry, ethical living, and the unity of existence offers valuable insights for navigating the complexities of contemporary existence.

In conclusion, while the Brahma Sutra is a deeply philosophical text, its teachings can be practically applied to enhance daily life, fostering personal growth, ethical behavior, and a deeper understanding of oneself and the world.

The Brahma Sutras have been a subject of extensive commentary and interpretation by various spiritual scholars throughout history, including in contemporary times. Here are detailed comments from some eminent contemporary spiritual scholars on the Brahma Sutras:

1. Swami Vivekananda:

While not strictly contemporary, Swami Vivekananda's influence extends into modern times. He said, "The Brahma Sutras are the head, the crest of the Vedanta philosophy." He emphasized that the Brahma Sutras provide a systematic and logical exposition of Vedantic thought, crucial for a deeper understanding of non-dualistic philosophy.

2. Swami Chinmayananda:

Founder of Chinmaya Mission, Swami Chinmayananda viewed the Brahma Sutras as essential for serious Vedantic students. He commented, "The Brahma Sutras serve as a bridge between the Upanishads and their practical application. They provide a logical structure to the seemingly diverse teachings of the Upanishads."

3. Dr. S. Radhakrishnan:

The philosopher and former President of India wrote extensively on the Brahma Sutras. He noted, "The Sutras are not so much systematized thought as the memoranda of systematized teaching. They give us only the headings, the contours of the system." He emphasized their role in codifying Vedantic thought.

4. Swami Sivananda:

Founder of the Divine Life Society, Swami Sivananda said, "The Brahma Sutras throw a searchlight on the Upanishads and remove the apparent contradictions in their teachings. They give a complete picture of the Vedanta philosophy." He stressed their importance in reconciling seemingly contradictory Upanishadic statements.

5. Sri Aurobindo:

Though primarily known for his integral yoga, Sri Aurobindo also commented on the Brahma Sutras. He observed, "The Sutras state the Vedanta philosophy in a series of brief aphorisms and form a sort of table of contents of the Upanishadic knowledge." He appreciated their concise nature and comprehensive scope.

6. Swami Paramarthananda:

A prominent contemporary Vedanta teacher, Swami Paramarthananda notes, "The Brahma Sutras are like a threading needle, stringing together the seemingly disparate beads of Upanishadic wisdom into a coherent necklace of knowledge." He emphasizes their role in systematizing Vedantic thought.

7. Dr. B.N.K. Sharma:

A renowned scholar of Vedanta, Dr. Sharma comments, "The Brahma Sutras represent the cream of Vedantic thought, offering a systematic and logical exposition of the ultimate reality." He highlights their philosophical rigor and depth.

8. Swami Sarvapriyananda:

A popular contemporary Vedanta teacher, Swami Sarvapriyananda says, "The Brahma Sutras are not just philosophical propositions, but a roadmap for the spiritual seeker. They provide both intellectual clarity and practical guidance for realizing the non-dual reality." He emphasizes their relevance to modern spiritual seekers.

9. Dr. Anantanand Rambachan:

Professor of Religion at St. Olaf College, Dr. Rambachan notes, "The Brahma Sutras play a crucial role in the Vedanta tradition by offering a systematic interpretation of the Upanishads and addressing philosophical objections to Advaita." He highlights their role in defending and clarifying Advaita philosophy.

10. Swami Dayananda Saraswati:

Founder of Arsha Vidya Gurukulam, Swami Dayananda said, "The Brahma Sutras are like a master key, unlocking the profound teachings of the Upanishads. They provide a logical framework for understanding the nature of reality, the self, and liberation." He emphasized their importance in Vedantic education.

11. Dr. David Frawley (Vamadeva Shastri):

An expert in Vedic studies, Dr. Frawley comments, "The Brahma Sutras represent the analytical side of Vedantic thought, complementing the more intuitive approach of the Upanishads. They show that spiritual knowledge can be precise and logical." He appreciates their analytical approach to spiritual truths.

12. Sri Sri Ravi Shankar:

Founder of the Art of Living Foundation, Sri Sri Ravi Shankar says, "The Brahma Sutras are not just ancient philosophy, but living wisdom that can transform our understanding of ourselves and the world. They provide a foundation for expanding our consciousness." He emphasizes their practical relevance in modern times.

These scholars generally agree on the Brahma Sutras' importance in systematizing Vedantic thought, reconciling apparent contradictions in the Upanishads, and providing a logical framework for understanding non-dual reality. They also highlight the Sutras' relevance to contemporary spiritual seekers, emphasizing their role in both intellectual understanding and practical spiritual growth.

Many of these scholars have written extensive commentaries or given detailed lectures on the Brahma Sutras, expanding on these brief comments. For a deeper understanding, one would need to study their more comprehensive works on the subject.

Appendix C : Brief Introduction To Bhagavad Gita

The Bhagavad Gita, often referred to as simply "the Gita," is a 700-verse Hindu scripture that is part of the Indian epic Mahabharata. It contains a conversation between Prince Arjuna and Lord Krishna, who serves as his charioteer and spiritual guide. The Gita provides numerous insights that are deeply relevant to our daily lives. Here are some key insights and their practical applications:

1. Karma Yoga: The Path of Selfless Action

Key Insight: The Gita teaches that we have the right to perform our prescribed duties, but not to the fruits of our actions. It emphasizes doing work for its own sake, without attachment to results.

Daily Life Application:

- Focus on putting in your best effort rather than worrying about outcomes.

- Perform your duties without expecting praise or rewards.

- Reduce stress and anxiety by detaching from the results of your actions.

2. Dharma: Duty and Righteousness

Key Insight: The Gita emphasizes the importance of fulfilling one's dharma or duty, even when it's challenging.

Daily Life Application:

- Identify and fulfill your responsibilities in various roles (e.g., professional, familial, social).

- Make ethical decisions based on what's right, not just what's easy or beneficial to you.

- Strive to maintain balance and harmony in your various life roles.

3. Self-Realization and True Nature of the Self

Key Insight: The Gita teaches that our true self (Atman) is eternal and unchanging, distinct from the physical body and mind.

Daily Life Application:

- Cultivate inner peace by understanding that your essential nature is beyond temporary circumstances.
- Practice self-reflection to distinguish between your true self and fleeting emotions or thoughts.
- Develop resilience in facing life's challenges by identifying with your unchanging essence.

4. Equanimity in Success and Failure

Key Insight: The Gita advises maintaining equilibrium in both favorable and unfavorable situations.

Daily Life Application:

- Practice emotional stability during both successes and setbacks.
- Avoid becoming overly elated or depressed due to external circumstances.
- Cultivate a balanced perspective on life's ups and downs.

5. Meditation and Self-Control

Key Insight: The Gita emphasizes the importance of meditation and controlling the mind.

Daily Life Application:

- Incorporate regular meditation or mindfulness practices into your daily routine.
- Practice self-discipline in thoughts and actions.
- Develop better focus and concentration in your work and personal life.

6. Bhakti Yoga: The Path of Devotion

Key Insight: The Gita presents devotion as a powerful spiritual path, emphasizing love and surrender to the Divine.

Daily Life Application:

- Cultivate gratitude and reverence in daily life.
- Practice selfless service as a form of devotion.
- Develop a sense of surrender to a higher power or purpose, which can reduce ego-driven stress.

7. Knowledge and Wisdom

Key Insight: The Gita distinguishes between mere information and true wisdom, emphasizing the importance of experiential knowledge.

Daily Life Application:

- Pursue not just academic or professional knowledge, but also wisdom that leads to personal growth.

- Apply what you learn in practical ways.

- Cultivate discernment in decision-making.

8. Gunas: The Three Qualities of Nature

Key Insight: The Gita describes three gunas (sattva, rajas, and tamas) that influence all aspects of nature and human behavior.

Daily Life Application:

- Recognize these qualities in yourself and strive to cultivate more sattva (purity, knowledge, harmony).

- Make conscious choices in diet, activities, and company to influence your mental state positively.

- Understand and manage your own tendencies and behaviors better.

9. Non-attachment

Key Insight: The Gita teaches the importance of non-attachment to material possessions and outcomes.

Daily Life Application:

- Practice letting go of things, relationships, or situations that no longer serve you.

- Reduce materialism and focus more on experiences and personal growth.

- Cultivate contentment with what you have.

10. Yoga as Skill in Action

Key Insight: The Gita defines yoga as "skill in action," emphasizing the importance of being fully present and skillful in whatever we do.

Daily Life Application:

- Strive for excellence in your work and daily tasks.

- Practice mindfulness in your actions.

- Develop a balanced, holistic approach to life that integrates body, mind, and spirit.

11. Universal Love and Compassion

Key Insight: The Gita promotes seeing the Divine in all beings and treating everyone with equal respect and compassion.

Daily Life Application:

- Cultivate empathy and kindness in your interactions with others.

- Practice non-judgment and acceptance of diversity.

- Engage in acts of service or volunteering to express universal love.

These insights from the Bhagavad Gita offer a comprehensive guide to living a meaningful, balanced, and spiritually rich life. By reflecting on these teachings and gradually incorporating them into daily life, one can potentially experience greater peace, purpose, and fulfillment. The Gita's wisdom is not meant to be merely understood intellectually but to be lived and experienced in our day-to-day existence.

The Bhagavad Gita has been widely studied, interpreted, and commented upon by numerous spiritual scholars and leaders throughout history. Here are some comments from eminent spiritual scholars on the Gita:

1. Mahatma Gandhi

"The Gita is the universal mother. She turns away nobody. Her door is wide open to anyone who knocks. A true votary of Gita does not know what disappointment is. He ever dwells in perennial joy and peace that passeth understanding."

2. Swami Vivekananda

"The Gita is a bouquet composed of the beautiful flowers of spiritual truths collected from the Upanishads."

3. Sri Aurobindo

"The Gita is not a weapon for dialectical warfare; it is a gate opening on the whole world of spiritual truth and experience and the view it gives us embraces all the provinces of that supreme region. It maps out, but it does not cut up or build walls or hedges to confine our vision."

4. Dr. S. Radhakrishnan (philosopher and former President of India)

"The Gita is not a system of philosophy, but a book for practical guidance in life. It is not so much a religious scripture as a spiritual manual."

5. Paramahansa Yogananda

"The Bhagavad Gita is the most beloved scripture of India, a scripture of scriptures. It is the Hindu's Holy Testament, the one book that all masters depend upon as a supreme source of scriptural authority."

6. Swami Chinmayananda

"The Gita is a text of deep spiritual wealth, and it needs to be read again and again, with devoted attention and a prayerful attitude to realize its profound wisdom."

7. Eknath Easwaran

"The Gita is not a book of commandments, but a book of choices. It does not tell us what to do; rather, it shows us our options and their consequences."

8. Osho

"The Gita is not a scripture belonging to any one religion. It is the very science of consciousness, and hence universal."

9. B.K.S. Iyengar (Yoga master)

"The Bhagavad Gita is not just a religious text, but a way of life. It teaches us how to live harmoniously with ourselves and with the world around us."

10. Ram Dass

"The Gita is a love song to reality, a text about awakening to the Divine in all beings and in oneself."

11. Dr. David Frawley (Vamadeva Shastri)

"The Bhagavad Gita remains ever relevant as it addresses the universal human dilemmas and shows a way to transcend them."

12. Swami Sarvapriyananda

"The Gita is a practical manual for transformation. It doesn't just give us knowledge, but shows us how to live that knowledge."

13. Sri Sri Ravi Shankar

"The Bhagavad Gita is a dialogue between the limited self and the unlimited self. It's about expanding our consciousness to embrace the totality of existence."

14. Sadhguru Jaggi Vasudev

"The Gita is not about devotion to Krishna; Krishna is only a representative. The Gita is about you taking charge of your life."

These diverse perspectives highlight the Gita's universal appeal and its ability to speak to people across different spiritual traditions and philosophical viewpoints. Many scholars emphasize its practical wisdom, its relevance to daily life, and its potential for personal transformation. They also often point out that the Gita's teachings transcend religious boundaries and offer insights applicable to all of humanity.

It's worth noting that these are complex thinkers with extensive writings on the Gita, and these brief quotes only scratch the surface of their interpretations and insights. For a deeper understanding, one would need to study their more comprehensive works on the subject.